Precious Dolls
to knit and sew

Precious Dolls
to knit and sew

Marianne J. Porteners

Dolls designed and worked by
Claire Willemsen

Kangaroo Press

Photography, patterns and graphs: A.C. Porteners
Title page art: Lesley Boston; motifs from
Persian Designs and Motifs for Artists and Craftsmen by Ali Dowlatshahi
(Dover Publications Inc.)

First published in 1995 by Kangaroo Press Pty Ltd
3 Whitehall Road Kenthurst NSW 2156 Australia
P.O. Box 6125 Dural Delivery Centre NSW 2158
Printed in China through GlobalCom Pte Ltd

CONTENTS

A doll from At the Country Fair; instructions appear on page 36

INTRODUCTION

Recapture the gentle romance of yesteryear with this enchanting craft! This book presents a collection of irresistible handmade dolls, complete with instructions, patterns and diagrams. Designed by Claire Willemsen, now 90, the fully knitted dolls are dressed in finery sewn from simple patterns. The dresses are decorated with lace, braid or cross-stitch embroidery, and their exquisite accessories are either sewn or crocheted. Ready-made accessories such as straw hats and baskets are also used, and decorated with ribbons, lace and flowers to add a personal touch.

Precious Dolls came about in response to many requests for patterns and information about Claire's work. It contains clearly set out step-by-step instructions, and can be attempted by needlework enthusiasts at all levels of expertise.

Here is a book that passes on a creative hobby, together with admirable skills, from one generation to the next. At the same time it provides wonderful ideas for low cost precious gifts that any daughter, grandchild or special friend would cherish.

We hope the following pages will inspire and bring much pleasure!

Marianne J. Porteners

PROFILE OF
THE DESIGNER

Claire Willemsen is a remarkable woman. Now 90 years old, she lives in joyous retirement at Wesley Gardens in Belrose, New South Wales. Throughout the years she has shared with others her love of life, along with her love of needlework. Prior to retiring five years ago, she had for eleven years been teaching highly successful tapestry classes at the Senior Citizens' Centre in Narrabeen, New South Wales. She refuses to dwell on the negatives of life, and her philosophy is to keep busy and look for the best in people. Students attending Claire's classes have profited from her natural ability to teach, encourage and to entertain.

For many years she has combined her love of needlework, crochet and knitting to create her exquisite dolls.

After an article about Claire and her dolls was published in the *Australian Women's Weekly* in 1992, she was inundated with letters from people all over Australia, expressing their delight in her work, and requesting additional patterns and information.

Claire still works tirelessly on her dolls and cross-stitch embroideries, constantly developing new ideas and designs. It almost seems a miracle that her 90-year-old eyes and fingers are keeping up with her agile mind. 'A creative hobby is the best tonic,' she maintains, 'as are all things bright and beautiful.'

Claire would like to dedicate this book to her great-grandchildren, Alexandra, Russell and Tasman, and to her dear friend and fellow craftswoman, Ida Coenen.

HELPFUL INFORMATION

Materials you will need

Knitting Yarns and Needles

The dolls are knitted from acrylic yarns, but any type of yarn can be used. For each doll you will need about 20 g ($^3/_4$ oz) 8-ply white yarn and a pair of 3.25 mm (No 10) needles, and about 10 g ($^1/_2$ oz) 4-ply skin-coloured yarn and a pair of 2 mm (No 14) needles. The dolls in the illustrations are worked from Patons Supersaver 8-ply, white 2261, and the faces, arms and legs from Patons 4-ply Feathersoft Bri-nylon, shade 1703. Always retain the skein label for future supplies, especially of your favourite skin colour!

Hair

Yarns used for hair should preferably be 4-ply or 5-ply wool. The hair of most of the dolls in the photographs is worked with oddments of 4-ply woollen yarns in different shades of beige-brown, grey and cream.

Features

The dolls' features are worked with two strands of DMC stranded embroidery cottons. Suggested colours for the eyes are grey 451, light blue 794, medium blue 798 or brown 435, and for the mouth red 349 or pink 961.

Filling

The bodies of the dolls are stuffed with polyester fibre filling. For the dolls without legs, the filling is kept in place at the base with a circle of strong white cardboard covered with a white crocheted circle.

The head is filled with a foam ball to create a firm background for working the hair and features. If the appropriate sized foam ball is difficult to obtain, use a light coloured bead instead, or fill the head with polyester fibre filling and take extra care with hair and features.

The arms and legs are fairly narrow, and the seams provide sufficient bulk to make filling unnecessary. White pipe cleaners are inserted into the arms so that they can be bent to the desired position.

Dresses and Trimmings

As the dolls are fairly small, fine polyester cotton/chintz fabrics are recommended, especially for beginners. Taffeta, with its rich, glossy look, has been used for some of the dolls, but because it is slippery to handle and frays easily, a little sewing experience would be an advantage before using it. To build up a collection of suitable fabrics, buy 20–30 cm (8"–12") of fabrics that take your eye when you seem them—in plain, flowered, dainty patterns, checks, dots or stripes.

The petticoats are made from 3.5 cm ($1^1/_4$") wide gathered lace, and the dresses trimmed with straight or gathered lace 0.5–2.5 cm wide ($^3/_{16}$"–1"). Buy different edged and patterned nylon laces in 1 m (36") lengths, remembering that white is most often used.

Round off your collection of fabrics and trimmings with pretty braids 50 cm–1 m long (18"–36"), and 1 m (36") pieces of polyester taffeta ribbons in colours to match your fabric collection, ranging in width from 2 mm to 10 mm ($^1/_{16}$" to $^3/_8$"). If narrow taffeta ribbon is unobtainable, use double-faced satin instead.

Accessories and Decorations

Many of the accessories are handmade. The umbrellas for the Fairy Godmothers and the Country Fair trio are sewn from dress fabric. The Flower Seller's hat, collar and cuffs, and the small bags used by the Bridesmaids and the Fairy Godmother are crocheted from knitting cotton and pearl cotton. Suitable yarns include DMC Coton Perle No 8 (worked with a 1.50 mm hook), Milford Soft 4-ply knitting-crochet cotton and Pellicano Pearl Cotton No 5 (both from Coats) (worked with a 2.50 mm hook).

Small bunches of ribbon roses, flowerbuds and green leaves, straw baskets and hats, and all kinds of knick-knacks and trinkets can be used as decorations or ready-made accessories. Tiny buttons, flat rhinestones, costume jewellery, flocked animals and birds, shiny bells, stars, miniature tea-sets and musical instruments, and dolls' house furniture such as chairs and tables, will all come in handy.

The haberdashery sections of large department stores, needlework and handicraft shops, gift shops, toy shops, and even newsagents, have yielded most of the treasures used in this book.

Craft Glue

Some of the trimmings and accessories are glued in place, and for certain projects the dolls and decorations are glued to a wooden base. Always use a clear-drying craft glue, and use glue sparingly. *Note:* Most glue containers are opened by cutting off a section of the top edge to form a hole: make sure you don't cut off too much, as the opening must be fairly small. To apply the glue, squeeze a few drops into a shallow plastic dish, and pick up small amounts with a toothpick or matchstick. After the glue has been applied, allow it to dry thoroughly, and use fingers or a hairclip to add pressure for a short while. Before closing the container with its separate top, carefully remove all glue in and around the opening, using a paper tissue.

Sewplus Craft Glue, available from Sewplus Pty Ltd in Castle Hill in New South Wales and Hobby Glue from Lincraft are clear-drying glues, and are both highly recommended.

Knitting, crochet and sewing techniques

Knitting

Casting On
1st stitch: make a slip knot and place the loop on the left-hand needle.
2nd stitch: insert right-hand needle through 1st stitch, fold yarn around needle, draw through and place on left-hand needle.
3rd stitch: insert right-hand needle between 1st and 2nd stitch, fold yarn around needle, draw through and place on left-hand needle.
4th and all following stitches: insert right-hand needle between two last-made stitches, fold yarn around needle, draw through and place on left-hand needle.

Knit Stitch
Keep yarn at back of work. Insert right-hand needle through front of stitch on left-hand needle. Fold yarn around right-hand needle, pull through, and slip the stitch off the left-hand needle.

Purl Stitch
Keep yarn at front of work. Insert right-hand needle from right to left through front of stitch on left-hand needle. Fold the yarn around the right-hand needle, pull through, and slip the stitch off the left-hand needle.

Increasing (making two stitches from one)
Knit or purl into stitch, but do not slip it off the left-hand needle; knit again into the back of the same stitch, then slip it off the left-hand needle.

Decreasing (turning two stitches into one)
In a knit row: insert right-hand needle through both the second and the first stitch on the left-hand needle. Fold yarn around needle, pull it through *both* stitches, and slip both stitches off left-hand needle.
In a purl row: insert right-hand needle from right to left through front section of both the first and second stitch on the left-hand needle. Fold yarn around needle, pull it through *both* stitches, and slip both stitches off left-hand needle.

Rib Stitch
Knit all rows.

Stocking Stitch
Knit on right side. Purl on wrong side.

Crochet

Chain Stitch
Make a slip knot and place loop on crochet hook. Draw yarn through loop to form first chain. Continue to work as many chains as needed.

Slip Stitch
Insert hook in stitch, draw yarn through both the stitch and the loop on the hook.

Double Crochet

Insert hook in 2nd chain from hook, catch yarn and draw through chain (2 loops on hook), place yarn around hook and draw through both loops on hook.

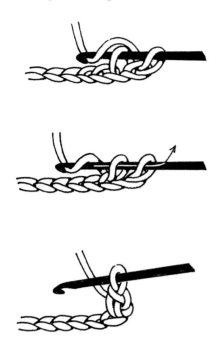

Treble

Place yarn around hook. Insert hook in 4th chain from hook, draw yarn through (3 loops on hook). Place yarn around hook, draw through two loops on hook, place yarn around hook, draw through two last loops on hook.

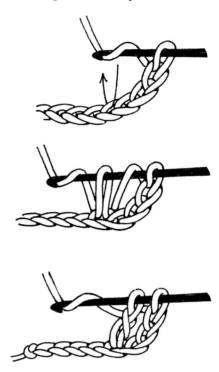

Cross-stitch embroidery

Some of the dolls' dresses are decorated with colourful borders in cross-stitch embroidery.

Cross-stitch is usually worked over evenweave fabrics. These fabrics are woven with the same number of fabric threads to the centimetre (inch) in length and width. Crosses are always worked in the same direction, e.g. with the top arm of each cross always from top left to lower right corner.

To work cross-stitches over the closely woven dress fabrics, use a piece of evenweave linen or waste canvas as a base. Baste the piece (slightly larger than the motif) over the area to be embroidered, and work through *both layers* of fabric, using a sharp pointed needle. Keep the needle perpendicular to the linen while working, and stitch only through the holes in the linen, not through the threads. When completed, carefully pull out the linen threads one by one with tweezers; if working with canvas, dampen it to soften it before withdrawing the threads.

Sewing

The dolls are fully handmade. If time is a factor, some of the dress seams could be sewn by machine, but because the dresses are fairly small, hand sewing is recommended, especially for beginners.

Only a few simple sewing stitches are needed throughout. Sewing and embroidery stitches are illustrated on the next page.

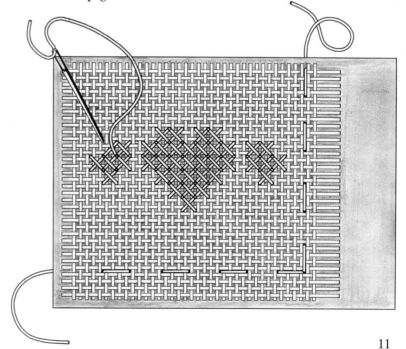

11

Stitch library

Sewing and Embroidery Stitches

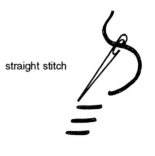

straight stitch

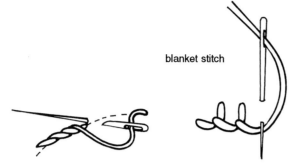

blanket stitch

stem stitch

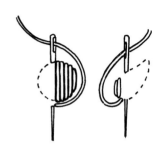

long and short stitch

satin stitch

running stitch

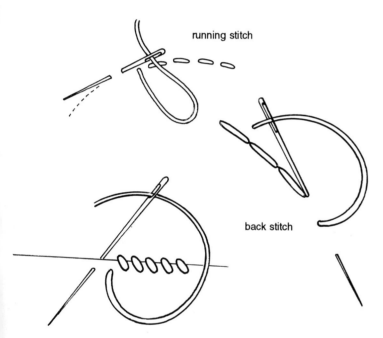

back stitch

whip stitch (overcast stitch)

cross stitch

slipstitch

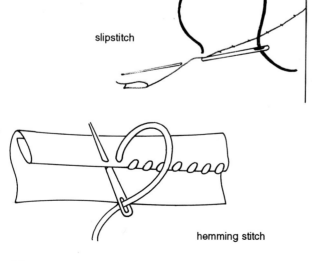

hemming stitch

Abbreviations

Knitting
cont = continue
dec = decrease
inc = increase
K = knit
K2tog = knit two together
P = purl
rem = remain/ing
rep = repeat
rib = knit all rows
st/s = stitches
st st = stocking stitch (knit
all sts on right side of work,
purl all sts on wrong side)
tog = together

Crochet
ch = chain
cont = continue
dc = double crochet
rep = repeat
rnd/s = round/s
sl st = slip stitch
sp = space
st/s = stitch/es
tog = together
tr = treble

BASIC METHOD

Knitting patterns

Measurements

The basic doll without legs comes in three sizes: large 20 cm (8"); medium 15 cm (6"); small 12 cm (4¾").
The small doll with legs is 12 cm (4¾") high.
See also Helpful Information on pages 9-12.
Knitting and crochet abbreviations appear on page 12.

Materials

Note: Measurements in brackets refer to medium and small dolls.

All dolls

Acrylic yarns: about 20 g (20 g, 15 g) 8-ply white, and 10 g (10 g, 8 g) 4-ply skin colour (pink)
Small quantities of 4-ply or 5-ply woollen yarns in desired colour for hair
Scraps of DMC stranded embroidery cottons for features
Small quantity polyester fibre filling
Clear-drying craft glue
One pair each 3.25 mm (No 10) and 2 mm (No 14) knitting needles
Large-eyed tapestry needle to work seams and hair
No 26 tapestry needle to embroider features

You will also need:
Basic doll (without legs)
4 cm (3 cm, 2.25 cm) diameter white foam ball (1½", 1¼", ⅞")
6 cm (5 cm, 4 cm) diameter strong cardboard circle (2⅜", 2", 1½"), and a crocheted circle the same size (see method below)
2 x 12 cm (5") white pipecleaners
12 cm (11 cm, 10 cm) diameter circle of dress fabric (4¾", 4½", 4")
60 cm (50 cm, 50 cm) x 3.5 cm (1¼") white gathered nylon lace for the petticoat (24", 20", 20")
Doll with legs
2.25 cm (⅞") diameter white foam ball
4 x 12 cm (5") white pipecleaners

10 cm x 25 cm (4" x 10") thin white fabric
10 cm (4") ungathered nylon lace for bloomers

Yarn Tension

10 sts and 16 rows to 3 cm (1¼") in stocking stitch, using 4-ply yarn and 2 mm (No 14) needles
7 sts and 10 rows to 3 cm (1¼") in stocking stitch, using 8-ply yarn and 3.25 mm (No 10) needles
Note: When starting work, changing colour of yarn or finishing work, always leave ends of yarn long enough for joining seams.

Pattern for Basic Doll

The doll is knitted in stocking stitch except for a small section at the base of the body knitted in rib. The body and head are worked in one piece, and the arms are worked separately. The doll has no legs, and is closed at the base with a cardboard and crocheted circle. The head is filled with a foam ball, the body with polyester fibre filling, and the arms with pipecleaners folded in half. The doll is finished with a 'petticoat' of dress fabric and layers of gathered lace.

Large doll

Body and head
Worked in one piece.
Using white and 3.25 cm (No 10) needles, cast on 30sts.
Work 8 rows in rib.
Work 34 rows st st, starting with a knit row.
Break off white. Change to pink and 2 mm (No 14) needles to work neck and head.

Neck/head
Work 5 rows st st to form neck.
Next row: P, and inc 2sts evenly across row for head (32 sts).
Work 24 rows st st, starting with a knit row.
Shape top of head
Next row: *K2tog*; rep from * – * to end of row (16sts).
Next row: *P2tog*; rep from * – * to end of row (8sts).
Break off yarn. Thread yarn end through 8 rem sts, draw up and fasten off.

Arms

Make 2. If preferred, work both arms at the same time on the same needle, using two small individual balls of yarn.

Using pink and 2 mm (No 14) needles cast on 6sts for each arm.

1st row: K, and inc 1st in each st (12sts).

Work 27 rows st st, starting with a purl row.

Cast off.

Medium doll

Body and Head

Using white and 3.25 mm (No 10) needles, cast on 28sts.

Work 6 rows in rib.

Work 34 rows st st, starting with a knit row. Break off white. Change to pink and 2 mm (No 14) needles to work neck and head.

Neck/head

Next row: K, and dec 2sts evenly across row (26sts).

Work 23 rows st st, starting with a purl row.

Shape top of head

Next row: *K2tog*; rep from * – * to end of row (13sts).

Next row: *P2tog*; rep from * – * to end of row (7sts)

Break off yarn, thread yarn end through 7 rem sts, draw up and fasten off.

Arms

Make 2. If preferred, work both arms at the same time on the same needle, using two small individual balls of yarn.

Using pink and 2 mm (No 14) needles, cast on 5sts for each arm.

1st row: K, and inc 1st in each st (10sts).

Work 25 rows st st, starting with a purl row.

Cast off.

Small doll

Body and head

Using white and 3.25 mm (No 10) needles, cast on 26sts.

Work 6 rows rib.

Work 26 rows st st, starting with a knit row. Break off white. Change to pink and 2 mm (No 14) needles to work neck and head.

Neck/head

Next row: K, and dec 3sts evenly across row (23sts).

Work 21 rows st st, starting with a purl row.

Shape top of head

Next row: *K2tog*; rep from * – * to end of row (12sts).

Next row: *P2tog*; rep from * – * to end of row (6sts).

Break off yarn, thread yarn end through 6 rem sts, draw up and fasten off.

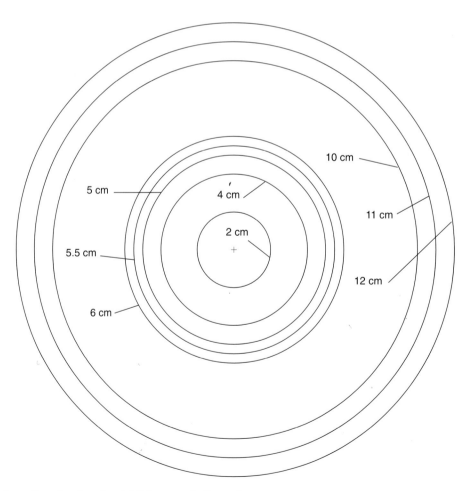

Handy circle guide for cardboard and crocheted doll bases, umbrellas and caps

Arms

Make 2. If preferred, work both arms at the same time on the same needle, using two small individual balls of yarn.

Using pink and 2 mm (No 14) needles, cast on 5sts for each arm.

1st row: K, and inc 1st in each of last 4sts (9sts).

Work 23 rows st st, starting with a purl row.

Cast off.

Crocheted circle for base

Work the same for all sizes, but cease working when the circle measures in diameter respectively 4 cm (1½") for small doll, 5 cm (2") for medium doll, 6 cm (2⅜") for large doll.

Using white yarn and 2.50 mm hook, make 4ch. Join with a sl st to form a ring. Cont in rnds, joining each rnd with a sl st.

1st rnd: 8dc around ring.

2nd rnd: 2dc in each dc (16sts).

3rd rnd: *1dc, 2dc in next dc*; rep from * – * to end (24sts).

4th rnd: *1dc in each of next 2dc, 2dc in next dc*; rep from * – * to end (32sts).

5th rnd: *1dc in each of next 3dc, 2dc in next dc*; rep from * – * to end (40sts).

Rep last rnd until circle measures desired diameter.

Pattern for small doll with legs

The doll is knitted in stocking stitch. The legs, body and head are knitted in one piece, and the arms are knitted separately. The head is filled with a foam ball, the body with polyester fibre filling, and the arms and legs with white pipecleaners folded in half. The doll is dressed in bloomers sewn from thin white cotton.

Legs

Make 2. If preferred, work both legs at the same time on the same needle, using two small individual balls of yarn.

Using pink and 2mm (No 14) needle, cast on 5sts for each leg.

1st row: K, and inc 1st in each st (10sts).

Work 23 rows st st, starting with a purl row. Break off pink and change to white using 3.25 mm (No 10) needles to start body.

Body

1st row: working over first leg, K4, inc 1st in next st, K5, cast on 2sts; working over second leg K4, inc 1st in next st, K5 (24sts).

Work 19 rows st st, starting with a purl row.

Break off white, change to pink and 2mm (No 14) needles to work neck and head.

Neck/head

Next row: K, and dec 3sts evenly across row (21sts).

Work 19 rows st st, starting with a purl row.

Shape top of head

Next row: *K2tog*; rep from * – * to end of row (11sts).

Next row: *P2tog*; rep from * – * to end of row (6sts).

Break off yarn, thread yarn end through 6 rem sts, draw up

and fasten off.

Arms

Make 2. If preferred, work both arms at the same time on the same needle, using two small individual balls of yarn.

Using pink and 2 mm (No 14) needles, cast on 5sts for each arm.

1st row: K, and inc 1st in each st (10sts).

Work 25 rows st st, starting with a purl row.

Cast off.

Assembly and filling

Note: When joining seams, sew white seam with white yarn, and pink seam with pink yarn.

Basic dolls

With right sides together, join arm seam, leaving shoulder end open. Turn to right side by placing the end of a knitting needle against the 'hand' and pulling the arm downwards over the needle, pushing the hand gently through. Finger-press the seam carefully. Fold a pipecleaner in half and insert it into the arm with the bend inside the hand. Trim the ends at the top edge even with the arm.

Repeat for other arm.

With right sides together, join back body and head seam. Turn to right side. Using pink yarn, stitch a row of small running stitches through the 5th row of pink on the neck. Insert foam ball, draw up gathering thread tightly and fasten off.

Fill the body, taking care not to stretch it out of shape. Mould the body while filling, especially around the top area to form shoulders.

Apply several very small dots of craft glue along the outer edge of the cardboard circle. Place it against the filling and slightly inside the base. Position the crocheted circle over the cardboard and using overcast stitch, sew the edge to the lower edge of the ribbed body base.

Working small overcast stitches, sew the arms along their rounded top edge to the body. Position the inside arm seam in line with the side of the body, and place the top edge of the arm against an imaginary shoulder seam, about 4 rows down from the gathering thread of the neck/head.

Petticoat

Sew a row of running stitches around the outside edge of the fabric circle for the petticoat. Centre the circle, right side out, over the base of the doll, then pull up the gathering thread to fit around the body. Fasten off. Lightly sew the edge of the fabric to the body, and sew gathered lace over the raw edge to cover it. Sew three more rows of gathered lace, one above the other, to form a petticoat.

Before you make the petticoat, fit the doll with her dress bodice/blouse so the lower edge can be hidden inside the petticoat.

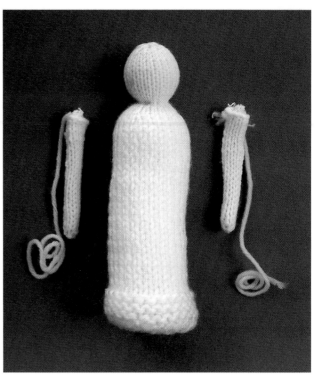

1. For the basic doll (without legs), the body and head are knitted in one piece, and the arms worked separately. You will also need a foam ball, polyester fibre filling, two pipecleaners, a cardboard circle and a crocheted circle

2. The remaining stitches of the head are drawn up. The body/head is sewn together to form a tube. The head is filled with a foam ball and the body with polyester fibre filling. The filling is kept in place at the base with the cardboard and crocheted circles. Each arm is sewn together to form a tube, and filled with a folded pipecleaner. The bent end of the pipecleaner goes inside the hand, and any surplus is cut even with the top of the arm

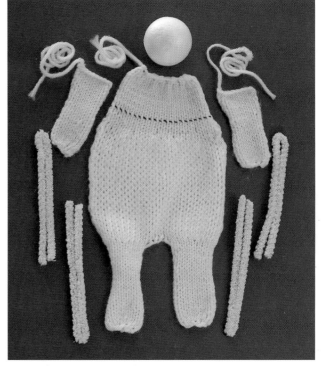

3. The arms are sewn to the body around their circular top opening, with the underarm seam positioned on the inside. A circle of dress fabric is sewn over the base of the doll. This is covered with two or three rows of gathered lace to form a petticoat

4. For the doll with legs, the body, head and legs are knitted in one piece, while the arms are worked separately

5. *The doll is assembled in the same way as the doll without legs, but without the circles at the base. Instead, the legs are sewn together and filled with pipecleaners like the arms. The petticoat is replaced by lace-edged bloomers*

in line with the side of the body, and place the top edge of the arm against an imaginary shoulder seam, about 4 rows down from the gathering thread for the head.

Bloomers

Copy the pattern for the bloomers onto tracing paper, and cut out the paper pattern. Lay the 10 cm x 25 cm (4" x 10") piece of fabric horizontally on the work-table. Fold both ends over to the centre until the raw edges just meet. Pin fabric to hold in place. Position the pattern on the doubled right-hand side of the fabric, matching the foldline with the fabric fold. Cut out the fabric piece. Turn the pattern over, and repeat for the left-hand side.

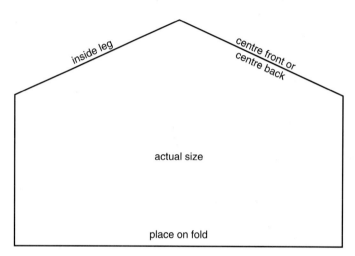

Pattern for bloomers, including 6 mm (¹/₄") seam allowances

Doll with legs

With right sides together, join arm seam, leaving shoulder end open. Turn to right side by placing the end of a knitting needle against the 'hand' and pulling the arm downwards over the needle, pushing the hand gently through. Finger-press the seam carefully. Fold a pipecleaner in half and insert it into the arm with the bend inside the hand. Trim the ends at the top edge even with the arm.

With right sides together, join the back of the head and about half of the back body seam, leaving the rest open for filling. Turn to right side. With right sides together, join leg seam. Turn to right side in same way as for the arm, placing the knitting needle against the 'foot'. Repeat for other leg.

Using pink yarn, sew a row of small running stitches through the 5th row of pink on the neck. Insert foam ball. Draw up gathering thread tightly and fasten off.

Fill the body, taking care not to stretch it out of shape. Mould the filling, especially around the top area to form shoulders.

Fold a pipecleaner in half and insert it in the leg with the fold inside the foot. Push the surplus length of pipecleaner inside the filling at the side of the body. Repeat for other leg. Close remaining back body seam with small overcast stitches.

Working small overcast stitches, sew the arms along their rounded top edge to the body. Position the inside arm seam

To assemble bloomers, sew the two pieces together along the centre front seams, the centre back seams, and both inside leg seams in one continuous row. Overcast the seam edges, and turn the pants to the right side. Sew lace around the lower edge of the legs, with the raw edge of the fabric turned under. Fit the bloomers on the doll, turning under the top edge, and sew the bloomers to the body. You may like to work a row of running stitches along the lower edge of the legs, and draw up to fit, forming a narrow fabric ruffle.

Hair and features

The techniques for hair and features are the same for all dolls, adapted only slightly for the different sizes. See also Helpful Information on pages 9-12.

Hairstyles

Basic Style

Using desired yarn and large-eyed tapestry needle, work a row of satin stitches 7.5–10 mm long (¹/₄"–³/₈") around the face and head. Start at one side of the face, about 7.5 mm (¹/₄") in front of and 5 mm (³/₁₆") below an imaginary

One plait across head

Hair with one plait at back

Hair with bun on top of head

'ear', working towards the other 'ear'. Work a second row in the same way, fitting the stitches into the previous ones, and following the shape of the head. Continue until the head is fully covered with yarn.

One plait across head

First make the basic style. For the plait, cut six 50 cm (20") lengths of 4-ply yarn. Using a large-eyed tapestry needle, thread these through the knitting at the base of the hairline, below the ear, so the centre of each thread is looped around one or two knitted stitches, and the threads are folded in two.

Divide them equally into three for plaiting. When the plait is long enough to fit across the head to just below the other 'ear', tie the end, trim excess yarn, and push the end under. Secure the plait to the head with a few stitches.

Hair parted in the middle with a bun

Thread a large-eyed tapestry needle with a long length of 5-ply yarn.

Starting about 8 mm ($^1/_4$") in front of and 5 mm ($^3/_{16}$") below one 'ear', work towards the centre above the fore-head. Take a small stitch (this will form the beginning of the parting), then work towards the other ear, and insert the needle about 8 mm ($^1/_4$") in front and 5 mm ($^3/_{16}$") below it. Return towards the parting and make a small stitch close to the first one, then work towards the starting point, working a small stitch close to the first stitch. Continue in this way until the parted hair covers about three-quarters of the head. Cover the rest of the head with long vertical satin stitches. To make the bun, cut six 50 cm (20") lengths of 5-ply yarn. Using a large-eyed tapestry needle, thread these through the knitting at the centre back of the head, so the centre of each thread is looped around one or two knitted stitches, and the threads are folded double. Divide the threads into three equal lots and make a plait. Tie the end and trim excess yarn. Roll the plait into a bun, push the end under, and sew the bun in place. Cover the stitchline of the parting with two long straight stitches.

Hair with bun on top of head

First make the basic style. Work the bun in the same way as the bun for the hair parted in the middle, but start the plait on the top of the head in the centre.

Hair with rolled plaits over ears

First work the basic style. Work two rolled plaits in the same way as the bun for the hair parted in the middle, but use only three strands of 4-ply yarn, and start each plait over an imaginary 'ear'.

Hair with one plait at back

First work the basic style. Work a plait in the same way as for the bun for the hair parted in the middle, but use 6 strands 4 or 5-ply yarn, and start the plait near the base of the hairline at centre back. When the plait is the desired length, tie a ribbon around it, cut excess yarn about 1 or 2 cm ($^1/_2$"–$^3/_4$") below the ribbon and fray the ends.

Features

Using a tapestry needle, work the eyes and mouth with two strands of embroidery cotton in the appropriate colours. Work each eye separately with about three small back stitches on top of each other. Work the mouth the same way a few rows below, exactly in the centre. Check the photographs for exact positions. When making the first back stitch, leave a short end of yarn at the beginning of the stitch. When the last stitch is completed, carefully cut the thread close to the embroidery, and cut the extended end, with small, sharp pointed scissors.

If you prefer, you can make the eyes from beads or very small pieces of felt, glued in place.

Dressing the dolls

Specific instructions for dressing and decorating individual dolls are included with each project.

Basic Dress Patterns

Each dress consists of a separate bodice and skirt. They can be worked from the same fabric to make a dress, or from two different coloured fabrics for a blouse and skirt. The bodice has either kimono sleeves or puffed sleeves.

The right and left backs are sewn together with slipstitch when the bodice is fitted on the doll. The bodice is not sewn to the skirt, but tucked inside the skirt for easy sewing. The skirt is made in one piece, with a seam at centre back.

6 mm ($^1/_4$") seam allowances are included on all patterns. Using tracing paper, trace the full sized patterns of the selected bodice in small, medium or large, and cut out the paper patterns.

Sew all pieces with right sides together. Cut away seam corners and clip seam curves. Tidy the seam edges with overcast stitches or cut with pinking shears, and press seams open.

Skirt: Following the skirt pattern layout on page 21, draw up the required measurements and cut out the paper pattern.

Note: Depending on personal knitting tension and manner of filling, the knitted doll may turn out slightly larger or smaller than anticipated and you may need to adjust the length of the skirt. To do this, measure the doll from waist to bottom, and add 1 cm ($^3/_8$") hem allowance (or 3 cm ($1^1/_4$") for an embroidered skirt), and 6 mm ($^1/_4$") seam allowance on the top edge. The width of the skirt remains as indicated on the layout.

Sewing Tips

Bodice with puffed sleeves: Sew the shoulder seams of front and backs. Gather the top edge of the sleeves to fit the armholes. Sew the sleeves inside the armholes.

Both bodices: Make a narrow hem along the lower edge of the sleeves. Join the sides of the bodice and inside sleeve seams in one continuous line. Hem the lower edge of the bodice. Make a narrow turning along the neck edge, and work a row of small running stitches to keep it in place: start and end the row about 5 mm ($^1/_4$") inside the top centre back edges, and leave the thread end long enough to draw up once the backs are sewn together. Fit the bodice on the doll. Make a narrow turning on the centre back edge of each back. With the turning-folds exactly meeting, sew the backs together with small slipstitches. Draw up the gathering thread to fit the neck edge, and fasten off. To make a sleeve ruffle, work a row of small running stitches 3-10 mm ($^1/_8$"–$^3/_8$") from the edge, and draw up to fit the arm or wrist.

Note: If the sleeve edges are to be decorated with lace, work the ruffle after the lace has been sewn on.

Skirt: Sew the centre back seam of the skirt. Hem the lower edge with a 5 mm ($^3/_{16}$") double hem; for the embroidered skirt make a 2 cm ($^3/_4$") hem with 1 cm ($^3/_8$") turned under. The waist edge does not have to be turned under, as it will be covered by the sash. Work a row of gathering stitches around the top edge. Fit the skirt on the doll over the bodice, and gather the top edge to fit around the waist. Staystitch in place with a few running stitches.

Pattern for bodice with puffed sleeves (actual size) includes 6 mm (¹/₄") seam allowance

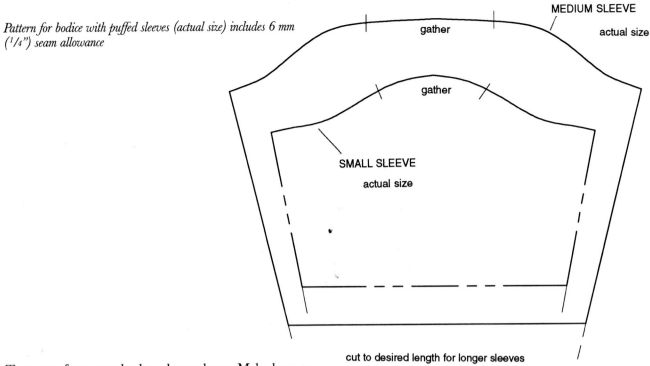

MEDIUM SLEEVE

actual size

gather

gather

SMALL SLEEVE

actual size

cut to desired length for longer sleeves

Trace one front, one back and one sleeve. Make long or short sleeves as preferred.

Cut one front, two sleeves, and two half backs (one reversed).

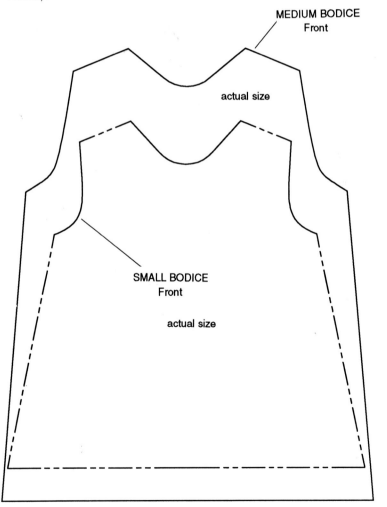

MEDIUM BODICE
Front

actual size

SMALL BODICE
Front

actual size

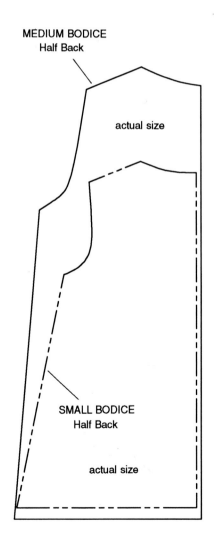

MEDIUM BODICE
Half Back

actual size

SMALL BODICE
Half Back

actual size

Pattern for bodice with kimono sleeves (actual size) includes 6 mm (¹/₄") seam allowance

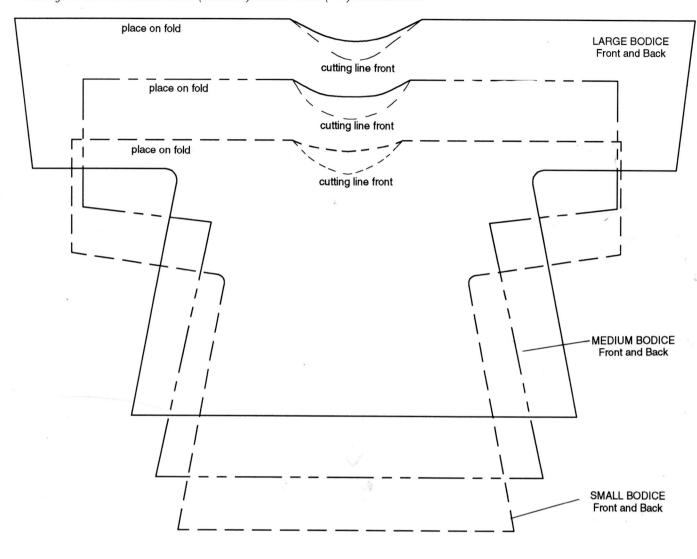

place on fold

LARGE BODICE
Front and Back

cutting line front

place on fold

cutting line front

place on fold

cutting line front

MEDIUM BODICE
Front and Back

SMALL BODICE
Front and Back

Trace one.
To cut, fold the fabric double. Pin the paper pattern to the fabric, matching the foldline with the fold of the fabric. Cut out the fabric piece. Cut the back vertically through the centre, forming two half backs. Cut the front neck edge following the broken line on the pattern.

Pattern for skirt includes 6 mm (¹/₄") seam allowances and 1 cm (³/₈") hem allowance

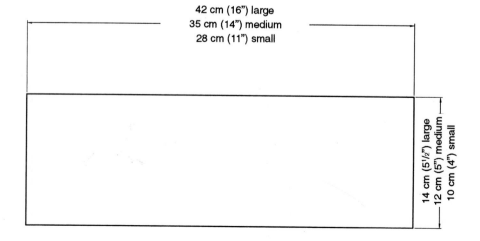

42 cm (16") large
35 cm (14") medium
28 cm (11") small

14 cm (5½") large
12 cm (5") medium
10 cm (4") small

THE PROJECTS

The materials and methods are described in detail for each project, showing how the basic patterns can be adapted to create a variety of individual dolls. We hope this will give you the confidence to design your own unique theme dolls. Fairy tales, music, poems, sports, hobbies and the professions provide all kinds of wonderful themes to fire the imagination. By simply adding or omitting a few stitches and rows of the basic knitting pattern, the dolls can be made in any desired shape and size. And for a particular individual touch, dress the dolls in fabrics left over from favourite garments, or in suitable pieces of your special worn-out ones! It goes without saying to always use your own favourite colours or colours loved by the recipient of your creation.

1: SELF-PORTRAIT

Finished Size

Doll 16 cm (6¼"); wooden base 14 cm (5½") diameter.

Materials

Following the instructions on pages 13-19, make a medium sized basic doll with white-dotted mauve petticoat and light beige hair with plait over head

25 cm x 115 cm of thin white-dotted mauve fabric (10" x 45")

Matching coloured sewing thread

Tracing paper

Pencil and ruler

Clear-drying craft glue

40 cm x 1.5 cm gathered white lace (16" x ⁵⁄₈")

40 cm x 7.5 mm mauve braid with white and grey flowers (16" x ¼")

Two small bows made from 3 mm (⅛") mauve ribbon

10 cm x 1 cm wide mauve satin ribbon for the sash (4" x ³⁄₈")

Count 14 Aida handwork fabric, 10 cm (4") square

Small quantities stranded embroidery cottons in green, rose and yellow

Tapestry needle

Small sewing box filled with yarns and scissors (if this is difficult to obtain, use any pretty small box, and fill it with tiny pieces of cardboard wound with embroidery yarns)

14 cm (5½") diameter circle of 10 mm (³⁄₈") thick wood, painted white

50 cm x 1 cm pretty edged ribbon (20" x ³⁄₈")

Dressing and decorating

Make a medium-sized skirt and bodice with kimono sleeves (see pages 20-21). Finish the lower edges of the sleeves with lace and a 5 mm (³⁄₁₆") wide ruffle.

For the collar cut 20 cm (8") gathered lace. Match the centre of the lace with the centre of the front neck edge. Sew the lace along the front and sides of the neck edge, forming a square neckline. Cross over the remaining lace at the back, trim surplus and glue the ends onto the raw top edge of the skirt at the back.

For the sash, glue a ribbon around the waist, covering the raw top edge of the skirt (and collar ends), and overlap

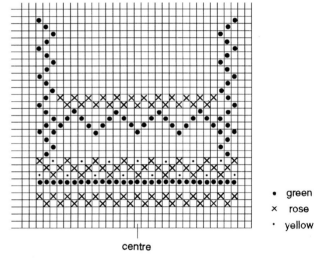

- • green
- × rose
- · yellow

centre

the ends of the ribbon at centre back. Sew flower braid along the lower edge of the skirt on the right side. Glue a small piece of flower braid over the lace collar at the front, and a small piece over the seam of the sash at the back.

Glue a mauve bow over the hair at the beginning and end of the plait.

Cross-stitch sampler: Following the graph and key, embroider the sampler motif in the centre of the Aida fabric. Work in cross-stitch over one fabric square, using two strands of embroidery cotton. When completed, cut the Aida cloth 8 squares outside the embroidery. Fold the top edge under along the outermost stitches of the embroidery, and turn under 5 mm (³⁄₁₆") along the sides and lower edge. Sew lightly in place with white sewing thread. Press the embroidery from the back under a damp cloth. Cut 15 cm (6") green embroidery cotton and knot one end. Insert the thread from back to front through the sampler near the top edge.

Bend the doll's arms into a realistic position, following the photograph. Glue the sampler under the left hand, and the loose end of the embroidery thread in the right hand. If necessary, glue the sampler lightly against the dress to keep it in place.

Glue ribbon around the outer edge of the wooden base. Glue the doll and the sewing box onto the base, positioning them as in the photograph.

For this self-portrait, Claire decided to dress up in her favourite colour, mauve, and do what she likes best beside creating dolls: cross-stitch embroidery! Such a doll would be a charming gift for someone who loves needlework. You could adapt the style and colour of the dress to the taste of the recipient

2: LITTLE GOOSE GIRL

Finished Sizes
Doll about 20 cm (8"), wooden base 16.5 cm (6½") diameter

Materials
Following the instructions on pages 13-19, make a large basic doll with blue flowered petticoat and light beige hair with rolled plaits over ears.

For the skirt/petticoat, 15 cm x 115 cm medium blue thin cotton fabric with small colourful flowers (6" x 45")

for blouse and apron, 20 cm x 115 cm (8" x 45") thin white fabric, and for apron ties 40 cm x 1 cm (16" x ³/₈") white taffeta ribbon

For apron embroidery, 5 cm x 14 cm (2" x 5½") linen with 11 fabric threads per 1 cm (or count 14 waste canvas); small quantities bright red, green and yellow stranded embroidery cottons; a sharp pointed needle

For the sleeve edges, 20 cm x 3 cm (8" x 1¼") ungathered white lace

For the bolero, 15 cm x 10 cm (6" x 4") black felt; two small white plastic flowers (or any preferred decoration); thin gold cord; a fine large-eyed needle
Four 4.5 cm (1¾") tall white flocked geese
15 cm (6") stick
Matching coloured sewing threads
Tracing paper
Pencil and ruler
Clear-drying glue

For the base, a 16.5 cm (6½") diameter white wooden circle, decorated along the outer edge with a 2 cm (³/₄") blue painted border with small white flowers and yellow dots; alternatively, decorate the base with pretty ribbon glued along the outer edge.

Dressing and decorating
Using fabric to match the petticoat, make a large skirt from blue fabric, and a large bodice with long kimono sleeves from white fabric (see pages 19-21). Finish the lower edge of the sleeves with lace and a 5 mm (³/₁₆") fabric ruffle.

Headband: Cut an 8 cm x 2 cm (3¼" x ¾") strip blue flowered fabric. Press all edges under 5 mm (³/₁₆"). Position the band over the head between the two rolled plaits, and glue in place.

Bolero: Trace the pattern on page 28 onto tracing paper and cut out. Pin the paper pattern over the black felt and cut out. Fold the fronts over on the shoulder lines and sew the short side seams. Fit the bolero on the doll. Close the bolero with thin gold cord, carefully lacing the cord through the front edges with a fine large-eyed needle, and tying the ends into a bow (see the photograph). Glue a small plastic flower or any other decoration onto each front.

Apron: (See Cross-stitch embroidery on page 11.) From white fabric cut one 16 cm x 14 cm (6¼" x 5½") apron piece, and one 8 cm x 3 cm (3¼" x 1¼") waistband. Baste the piece of linen or waste canvas over one long side of the apron (the finished border should be 4.5 cm (1¾") above the lower raw edge of the skirt). Following the graph and colour key, embroider the border in cross-stitch, matching the centre with centre of apron. Work the crosses through both layers over two linen threads using two strands of embroidery cotton. Keep the needle perpendicular to the linen while working and stitch only through the linen holes, not the linen threads. When completed, cut away surplus linen and remove threads one by one with tweezers. Press the embroidery lightly on the wrong side.

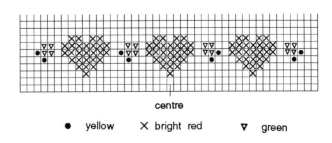

Embroidery graph for apron

Here is a gorgeous decoration with a rustic charm. The Little Goose Girl wears a bolero made from felt, and a white cotton apron decorated with cross-stitch embroidered hearts. The doll is 20 cm (8") tall and the geese measure 4.5 cm (1³/₄"). They are glued onto a wooden base, decorated with white and yellow flowers painted over a blue outer border. If preferred, decorate the base with pretty ribbon instead

27

Hem the sides of the embroidered piece with a 1 cm (³⁄₈") double hem, and the lower edge with a 2 cm (³⁄₄") double hem. Gather the top edge to measure 7 cm (2³⁄₄"). Using a 5 mm (¹⁄₄") seam, sew the waistband to the gathered edge with right sides together, raw edges even and centres matched. Turn under 5 mm (³⁄₁₆") on all sides and fold the band double. Using slipstitch, sew the band in place against the back of the apron over the previous stitchline.

Cut the taffeta ribbon in half to make two 20 cm (8") pieces. Making a narrow turning, sew one piece to each end of the waistband. Fit the apron on the doll, covering the raw top edge of the skirt. Glue lightly in place. Tie the apron strings into a bow at centre back. Glue the stick in the doll's left hand.

Glue the doll and geese onto the wooden base in the positions shown in the photograph.

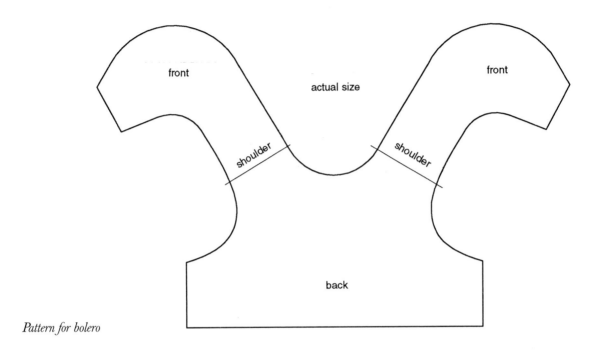

Pattern for bolero

3: MAYPOLE DANCE

Finished Size

Dolls 12 cm (4³/₄"); maypole 30 cm (12") high; wooden base 30 cm (12") diameter

Materials

Following the instructions on pages 13-19, make five small basic dolls with petticoat, features and hair: one doll with a flowered petticoat and plait at back tied with a pink bow; one doll with a white-dotted blue petticoat and rolled plaits over ears; three dolls with respectively white-dotted pink, blue, and mauve petticoats and a plait over the head.

For dresses and petticoats, five 20 cm x 115 cm (8" x 45") pieces thin fabric in white, small flowered white, white-dotted pink, blue, and mauve.

For apron, 8 cm (3¹/₄") square thin pink fabric and 20 cm x 1 cm (8" x ³/₈") matching taffeta ribbon for ties

Matching coloured sewing threads
Tracing paper
Pencil and ruler
Clear-drying glue

To decorate the five dolls

For white, pink, blue and mauve dresses:
30 cm x 2 cm (12" x ³/₄") gathered white lace; 30 cm x 7.5 mm (12" x ¹/₄") pretty flower braid to match fabric; 30 cm x 1 cm (12" x ³/₈") taffeta ribbon for dress sash (pink for the white doll and white for the three remaining dolls); 20 cm x 2 cm (8" x ³/₄") gathered white lace for the collar
1 m x 1 cm (36" x ³/₈") white ungathered lace for the lower sleeve edges
20 cm x 3 mm (8" x ¹/₈") blue and mauve ribbon and 40 cm x 3 mm (16" x ¹/₈") pink ribbon for small bows
One 5 cm (2") diameter and two 9 cm (3¹/₂") diameter straw hats
Small amounts of 7.5 mm (¹/₄") wide pretty flower braid to decorate the hats (same braid used to decorate dresses)
Two small mother-of-pearl buttons
Four small flat rhinestones

A necklace made from a silver four-leaf-clover charm laced onto silver thread
For the head of the doll with pink apron, 15 cm x 3 mm (6" x ¹/₈") white ribbon, and 7 pink and 7 white 7.5 mm (¹/₄") diameter ribbon roses

For the heads of the four remaining dolls, and the sash of the pink doll, a total of 10 white, 7 pink and 2 mauve 7.5 mm (¹/₄") diameter ribbon roses

For the maypole:
25 cm x 1 cm diameter (10" x ³/₈") white dowelling
30 cm (12") diameter circle of 1.5 cm (⁵/₈") thick wood, painted white, with a hole drilled in the centre to fit the dowel
8 cm (3") diameter green Oasis ball
Five 25 cm x 1 cm (10" x ³/₈") pale pink ribbons
Five dressmakers' pins
Several flower bouquets to yield a mixture of about 60 medium to small sized pink and white rosebuds with green leaves, and about 40 green sprigs with tiny pink flowers and buds: all these should have 2.5 cm (1") wire stems. Or use wired flowers and leaves of your choice (fabric or dried) to make the decorated top of maypole.

Dressing and decorating the dolls

For each doll select fabrics to match their petticoats, and make a small sized bodice and skirt following the instructions on pages 19-21. Select the bodice with kimono sleeves or puffed sleeves, and make long or short sleeves as preferred. For all dolls except the blue doll, finish the lower edge of the sleeves with lace and a narrow fabric ruffle.

Doll with flowered dress and pink apron

Glue two buttons to the front of the bodice.

Apron: Make 5 mm (³/₁₆") wide double hems around three sides of the pink fabric. Gather the raw edge (top side) to measure 4.5 cm (1³/₄"). Matching the centres, glue this edge to the front waist of the doll over the raw edge of the skirt. Matching the centre of the ribbon with the centre of the apron, arrange the ribbon (ties) around the waist, covering

Celebrate the return of spring with this delightful bunch of merrymakers, ready to dance and sing around the maypole and weave pretty patterns with ribbons that stream down from the top. This truly delightful decoration will bring a bit of spring into your home all year through!

This view reveals that attention to detail is just as important at the back of the dolls as at the front

the glued edge of the apron and top edge of the skirt. Glue the ribbon lightly in place, and tie the ends into a bow at the back.

Head: Take 15 cm of 3 mm (6" x ⅛") white ribbon, and glue 7 pink and 7 white small ribbon roses, alternating the colours, in the centre of the ribbon. Glue this flower band into a circle over the head, cutting off excess ribbon. Using 3 mm (⅛") pink ribbon, make two tiny bows, and glue these to the hair on each side of the head inside the band.

White, blue, pink and mauve dolls
For each doll, sew gathered lace around the lower edge of the skirt on the right side, and sew flower braid over the top edge of the lace.

Collars and necklace: For the collars of the white, pink and mauve dolls, cut an 18 cm (7") piece gathered lace. Match the centre of the lace with the centre of the front neck edge of the dress. Sew the lace around the front and sides of the neck edge, forming a square neckline. Cross over the remaining lace at the back, trim surplus, and glue the ends onto the raw top edge of the skirt at the back. Glue tiny bows over the corners of the collar at the front: pink for the white and pink dolls, mauve for the mauve doll. For the collar of the blue doll, use a 10 cm (4") piece gathered lace. Make narrow hems on both short ends, and sew the collar around the neck edge from centre back to centre back. Glue two flat rhinestones to the front and back of the collar (see photograph on page 30). Tie the four-leaf-clover necklace on the mauve doll.

Sashes: Glue the ribbon for the sash around the waist, covering the raw top edge of the skirt and the collar ends. Tie the ribbon into a bow at the back, making small loops and long ties: use pink ribbon for the white doll, and white ribbon for the mauve, pink and blue dolls. Glue a pink ribbon rose in the centre of the bow for the pink doll.

Hats and heads: Glue flower braid around the brims of the hats. Lightly glue the large hats to the heads of the mauve and the white dolls, bending the brims into pleasing shapes. Glue a ribbon rose over the hair over each imaginary ear directly below the hat: mauve for the mauve doll, and pink for the white doll.

For the pink doll, glue one white and two pink ribbon roses over the hair over each imaginary ear. For the blue doll, glue five white ribbon roses over the front, and three over the back of the head, forming a circle, and glue a tiny blue bow on each side between the two sections. Glue the small hat in the doll's left hand.

Maypole
Glue the dowel into the hole in the circular base. Leave to dry thoroughly. Apply glue over about 4 or 5 cm (1½"- 2") of the top end of the dowel and press the Oasis ball over the dowel; push and twirl it *gently* downwards over the glued area. Leave to dry thoroughly.

Make a narrow turning on one end of each of the 5 pieces of ribbon. Using a pin and glue, secure the pieces, evenly spaced, to the bottom of the Oasis ball, close to the pole. Starting from the base and working upwards, cover the Oasis ball with greenery, rosebuds and flower sprigs. Apply a small amount of glue to the flower wire, push the wire gently but firmly into the ball and leave to dry thoroughly.

To finish
Following the photographs, arrange and glue the dolls over the wooden base of the maypole. Bend their arms and hands into realistic positions. Straighten the 5 ribbon pieces hanging downwards from the base of the Oasis ball, determine the area that will fit inside the right hand of each doll, glue this section into the doll's hand, and leave to dry. Allow the ribbon ends to extend down about 5.5 cm (2¼") from the hands, and cut off surplus ribbon at an angle. Bend the hands slightly inwards to make it appear that the dolls are holding the ribbons.

4: FLOWER SELLER

Finished sizes
Doll about 17 cm (6³/₄"); wooden base 9 cm (3¹/₂") diameter.

Materials
Following the instructions on pages 13-19, make a medium basic doll, with black/white striped petticoat, features and basic hairstyle. *Note:* When knitting the doll, add 8 more rows to the white body to make the doll about 2 cm (³/₄") taller for a more elegant look.

20 cm x 115 cm (8" x 45") thin cotton with a narrow black/white stripe

Matching coloured sewing thread

Tracing paper

Pencil and ruler

Clear-drying glue

For the hat, a small quantity unbleached Coats Milford Soft 4-ply knitting-crochet cotton

For the cuffs and collar, a small quantity Coats Pellicano Pearl Cotton No 5

2.50 mm crochet hook

For the hat band, about 15 cm x 3 mm (6" x ¹/₈") brown ribbon or soft leather

Basket 2 cm high x 8 cm long with 6 cm handle (³/₄" x 3¹/₄", 2¹/₂")

A mixture of fabric flowers and green leaves, and a bouquet made from a few flowers and green leaves on 14 cm (5¹/₂") green stems

For the necklace, a small golden heart chart, laced onto a short length of thin gold thread

9 cm (3¹/₂") diameter circle of 7.5 mm (¹/₄") thick wood, painted white, and 40 cm x 7.5 mm (16" x ¹/₄") brown satin ribbon

Dressing and decorating the doll
Make a medium sized skirt and bodice with kimono sleeves from the black/white striped fabric (cutting the skirt about 2 cm (³/₄") longer), following the instructions on pages 19-21, and fit to the doll. For the sash, cut a 2.5 cm x 11 cm (1" x 4¹/₂") bias strip from the black/white striped fabric. Press under 5 mm (³/₁₆") on one short and two long sides. Glue the sash around the waist, covering the raw top edge of the skirt, and overlap the ends at centre back.

Crocheted hat
Refer to page 12 for crochet abbreviations.

Using unbleached cotton and 2.50 mm hook, work 4 ch, close into a ring with a sl st.

1st rnd: 8dc in ring. Use a safety-pin or tie a small piece of coloured thread through work to indicate the first stitch of the next rnd; move this at the beginning of each following rnd.

2nd rnd: 2dc in each dc (16 sts).

3rd rnd: *1dc, 2dc in next dc*; rep from * − * to end (24 sts).

4th rnd: *1dc in each of next 5dc, 2dc in next dc*; rep from * − * to end (28 sts).

5th rnd: *1dc in each of next 6dc, 2dc in next dc*; rep from * − * to end (32 sts).

7th − 11th rnd: Work in dc.

12th rnd: *2ch, miss 1dc, 1dc in next dc*; rep from * − * to end.

13th rnd: *2ch, 1dc in 2 ch loop*; rep from * − * to end.

14th rnd: *3 ch, 1dc in 2 ch loop*; rep from * − * to end.

15th rnd: *4ch, 1dc in 3ch loop*; rep from * − * to end. Fasten off.

Position the hat on the head and glue lightly in place. Glue ribbon or leather band around the brim, crossing the ends so they extend about 2 cm (³/₄") at centre back. Fold the brim around the face.

Crochet collar
Using Pearl Cotton and 2.50 mm hook, work a foundation row of 19ch.

1st rnd: 1dc in each ch.

2nd rnd: 1dc in next 9dc, miss 1dc, 1dc in next 9dc (18 sts).

3rd rnd: Work in dc.

4th rnd: *2ch, 1dc in next dc*; rep from * − * to end. Fasten off.

Sew foundation edge of **collar** to neck edge of dress, from centre front to centre front.

This beguiling creation is the perfect gift of love for someone dear! She is ideal for a birthday, engagement, anniversary or any other celebration, adapting the dress and flowers to the occasion. The doll's hat is crocheted from unbleached cotton, and the striped dress has a collar and cuffs crocheted from white pearl yarn. The necklace is a bracelet charm, laced onto a piece of gold thread

Crocheted cuffs

Make 2. Using Pearl Cotton and 2.50 mm hook, work 14ch;
   close into a ring with a sl st.
1st rnd: 1dc in each ch.
2nd rnd: Work in dc.
3rd rnd: *2ch, 1dc in next dc*; rep from * – * to end. Fasten off.
Slide the cuffs over the sleeve edges and sew in place along
   the foundation edge.

Tie the necklace around the doll. Glue brown ribbon
around the outer edge of the base and glue the doll on top
of the base in the centre.

Fill the basket with a pretty flower arrangement, gluing
the flowers in place. Bend the arms into a realistic position.
Glue the basket handle over the left hand, and the bouquet
in the doll's right arm.

Back view of dress and crocheted hat

5: AT THE COUNTRY FAIR

Finished sizes
Large dolls about 20 (8") cm; small doll about 12 cm (5")

Materials
Following the instructions on pages 13-19, make one small and two large basic dolls, with features, hair and petticoats; for the small doll make a pink/white checked petticoat and light beige hair with a plait over the head; for one large doll make a pale blue petticoat and grey hair with rolled plaits over imaginary ears; for the other large doll make a pink/white checked petticoat and dark beige hair with rolled plaits over imaginary ears.

For dresses and petticoats:
30 cm x 115 cm (12" x 45") pink/white checked fabric, and 25 cm x 115 cm (10" x 45") pale blue fabric
For aprons and umbrella, 15 cm x 115 cm (6" x 45") thin white fabric
Matching coloured sewing threads
Tracing paper
Pencil and ruler
Clear-drying glue

To decorate the large pink doll:
Three small mother-of-pearl buttons
70 cm x 1 cm (27" x $^3/_8$") ungathered white lace
30 cm x 1.5 cm (12" x $^5/_8$") gathered white lace
Three small bows made from 2 mm ($^1/_{16}$")white ribbon
For the umbrella, one 12 cm (5") white pipecleaner covered with white ribbon, with ribbon ends glued in place
9 cm (3$^1/_2$") diameter straw hat; 25 cm x 7.5 mm (10" x $^1/_4$") pink ribbon; two pink flowers with green leaves
For the apron, small quantities pink, green and yellow stranded embroidery cottons; 14 cm x 5 cm (5$^1/_2$" x 2") linen with 11 fabric threads per 1 cm (or count 14 waste canvas); 40 cm x 1 cm (16" x $^3/_8$") white taffeta ribbon for apron ties; a sharp pointed needle

To decorate the large blue doll:
Two small mother-of-pearl buttons
20 cm x 3 mm (8" x $^1/_8$") red ribbon
16 cm x 7.5 mm (6$^1/_2$" x $^1/_4$") red satin ribbon
9 cm (3$^1/_2$") diameter straw hat; 20 cm x 7.5 mm (8" x $^1/_4$")

red taffeta ribbon; three small colourful flowers and green leaves
Small quantities stranded embroidery cottons (see colour keys on the two graphs); linen with 11 fabric threads per 1 cm (or count 14 waste canvas)—two pieces 12 cm x 5 cm, one piece 7 cm x 5 cm, one piece 40 cm x 5 cm (5" x 2", 2$^3/_4$" x 2", 16" x 2"); a sharp pointed needle
Small quantity bright green DMC No 8 Coton Perle and a 1.50 mm crochet hook

To decorate the small doll:
Three small mother-of-pearl buttons
20 cm x 1 cm (8" x $^3/_8$") white taffeta ribbon
20 cm x 1 cm (8" x $^3/_8$") white ungathered lace
Two small bows made from 3 mm ($^1/_8$") pale pink ribbon
9 cm (3$^1/_2$") diameter straw hat; 14 cm x 7.5 mm (5$^1/_2$" x $^1/_4$") pale pink ribbon; four 1 cm ($^3/_8$") diameter pink ribbon roses
Basket 5 cm wide x 3 cm high with 3 cm handle (2" x 1$^1/_4$" x 1$^1/_4$")

Dressing the dolls
For each doll select fabric to match its petticoat, and make a bodice and skirt as described on pages 19-21.

For the small doll make a small skirt and bodice with puffed sleeves, with a 5 mm ($^1/_4$") fabric ruffle along the lower sleeve edges.

For the large pink doll make a large skirt and bodice with kimono sleeves, and finish the lower edge of the sleeves with 1.5 cm ($^5/_8$") gathered lace and a 1 cm ($^3/_8$") ruffle.

For the large blue doll make a large skirt and bodice with kimono sleeves, but add 3 cm (1$^1/_4$") hem allowance to the lower skirt edge. Before cutting out the bodice, work the embroidery and crocheted neck edging as follows (see Cross-stitch on page 11):

First make a paper pattern of the complete bodice (front and back). Fold a piece of paper double, trace the pattern, matching the fold of the paper with the foldline of the pattern, and cut out. Fold the pattern open. Making running stitches, outline the complete pattern onto the blue fabric. With centres matched, baste the 12 cm (5") pieces of linen over the foldline of the sleeves, and the 7 cm (2$^3/_4$") piece over the centre of the front bodice.

This good-looking trio is off to the country fair. They are dressed in their best finery and wear sensible straw hats. Mum has brought her lace-edged umbrella along, just in case. The little girl's basket will soon be filled with treats – Grandma is sure to spoil her little sweetheart

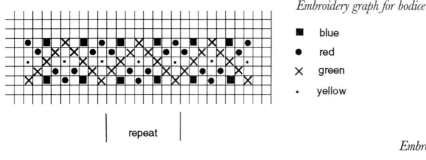

Embroidery graph for bodice

■ blue
● red
✕ green
· yellow

repeat

Embroidery graph for skirt

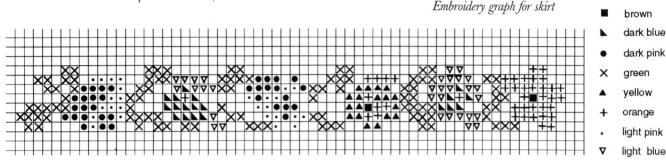

■ brown
◣ dark blue
● dark pink
✕ green
▲ yellow
+ orange
· light pink
▽ light blue

Following the graphs, embroider the borders through both layers in the centre of the linen, staying within the marked outlines of the bodice. Work in cross-stitch over two linen threads, using two strands of embroidery cotton. When completed, cut away surplus linen, and remove the linen threads one by one with tweezers. Cut out the bodice on the marked lines, and cut the back in half through the centre. Make a narrow hem on the lower edge of the sleeves. Fold the bodice double on the foldline with right sides together. Sew the sides and inside sleeves seams in one continuous line and clip the seam curves. Hem the bodice.

Crocheted neck edging

To form a foundation row for the crochet work, make a narrow turning along the neck edge, and using green Coton Perle embroider a row of 3 mm (¹/₈") blanket stitches, working the stitches 3 mm (¹/₈") apart. Work the crochet as follows:
1st row: Using green Coton Perle and a 1.50 mm crochet hook, work 1dc in each blanket st.
2nd row: 1tr, 2ch, *miss 2dc, 1tr in next dc, 2ch*; rep from * – * to end. Fasten off.

Fit the bodice on the doll. Close centre back of bodice and crocheted edging. Thread narrow red satin ribbon through the edging from centre front to centre front. Draw up and tie the ribbon in a small bow.

Embroidered skirt

Work the embroidered border for the skirt in the same way as for the bodice, omitting the running stitched outlines. Baste the 40 cm (16") piece of linen 2 cm (⁵/₈") above the lower edge of the skirt, and work the embroidered border in the centre of the linen through both fabric layers.

Note: The border should lie 4 cm (1¹/₂") above the lower raw edge of the skirt when the linen threads are removed.

Make a 2 cm (³/₄") hem with 1 cm (³/₈") turned under along the lower edge of the skirt. Finish the skirt and fit it on the doll following the instructions on pages 19-21.

Decorating the dolls

Large pink doll

Sew 1 cm (³/₈") ungathered lace along the lower edge of the skirt on the outside. Cut 20 cm (8") ungathered lace and sew the ends together. Work a row of small running stitches around the straight edge. Fit the collar on the doll, and draw up to fit around the neck. Glue two buttons to the centre front bodice, and one to the centre back top edge. Glue small bows over the stitchlines in the centre of the sleeve ruffles, and glue a bow over the top edge of the collar in centre front.

Make an apron for the doll as for Little Goose Girl on page 26, but work pink hearts instead of red hearts. Fit the apron on the doll.

Glue pink ribbon around the brim of the hat, crossing the ends at centre back and allowing 7 cm (2³/₄") of ribbon to hang free. Cover the ribbon-crossing with pink flowers and green leaves glued in place. Glue the hat over the head of the doll.

Umbrella

Cut an 11 cm (4¹/₂") diameter circle white fabric. Press under the raw edge of the circle. Sew gathered lace around the edge on the wrong side. Work a row of running stitches 1 cm (³/₈") inside the edge.

Push 1.5 cm (⁵/₈") of the ribbon-covered pipecleaner through a small hole in the centre of the fabric circle. Sew the hole closed to keep the pipecleaner in place. Draw up the gathering thread and fasten off. Glue a small piece of lace around the point to cover the sewing. Bend the top of the pipecleaner to form a handle and hang it over the bent right arm of the doll. Glue lightly in place.

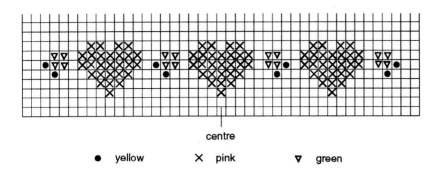

centre

● yellow   ✕ pink   ▼ green

Large blue doll

Cut a 12 cm x 2 cm (4³/₄" x ³/₄") blue fabric strip. Press under 5 mm (¹/₄") of two long sides and one short side. Glue the sash over the skirt around the doll's waist, overlapping the ends at centre back. Make a bow of 7.5 mm (¹/₄") red satin ribbon, and glue this over the seam of the sash. Glue two buttons over the centre back seam of the bodice. Glue taffeta ribbon around the brim of the hat, crossing the ends at centre back, allowing 4 cm (1¹/₂") ends to hang free. Cover the ribbon-crossing with three flowers and leaves glued in place. Glue the hat on the doll's head.

Small pink doll

Glue two buttons to the centre of the front bodice, and glue one button to the centre back top edge. Glue a small pink bow on the hair at each end of the plait. Glue pink ribbon around the brim of the hat, overlapping the ends at centre back. Glue three pink ribbon roses over the front of the hat band, and one over the seam at the back.

For the apron, cut a 10 cm x 6.5 cm (4" x 2⁵/₈") piece of white cotton. Hem one long and two short sides with 5 mm (³/₁₆") wide double hems. Sew lace around the hemmed edges on the inside. Gather the raw top edge to measure 5 cm (2"). Matching the centres, glue the top edge over the skirt at the waist. Matching the centres, glue the white ribbon tie around the waist, covering the gathered edge of the apron and remaining raw edge of the skirt. Make a bow at the back, forming small loops and long ties. Bend the doll's left arm and glue the handle of the basket over the left hand.

Bend the dolls' arms into realistic positions and hook the blue doll's right arm through the large pink doll's left arm. Stretch the right arm of the small doll to hold the left 'hand' of the blue doll. See the photographs.

6: THE KNITTING LESSON

Finished sizes

Large doll 20 cm (8"); small doll 12 cm (4³/₄")

Materials

Following the instructions on pages 13-19, make one large and one small basic doll, with petticoat and features; for the large doll make a blue patterned petticoat and grey hair parted in the middle with a bun; for the small doll make a cream patterned petticoat and light beige hair with a plait over the head. For dresses/petticoats, thin cotton fabrics with small colourful flower print: 25 cm x 115 cm (10" x 45") in dark blue, and 10 cm x 115 cm (4" x 45") in cream.

For aprons and cuffs, 10 cm x 115 cm (4" x 45") thin white cotton

For apron ties, white taffeta ribbon: 25 cm x 7.5 mm (10" x ¹/₄") and 40 cm x 1 cm (16" x ³/₈")

Matching coloured sewing threads

Tracing paper

Pencil and ruler

Clear-drying glue

To decorate the dolls

40 cm x 1.25 cm (16" x ¹/₂") white ungathered lace

Two small bows made from 3 mm (¹/₈") white ribbon

Two 7.5 mm (¹/₄") diameter mother-of-pearl buttons

Small quantity DMC Coton Perle No 8 and a 1.50 mm crochet hook

For knitting needles, six 6 cm (2¹/₂") toothpicks or beaded pins

Scraps of different coloured knitting yarns

Basket 3 cm high, 5 cm in diameter (1¹/₄", 2")

For the base of the small doll, a 9.5 cm (3³/₄") diameter circle of 1 cm (³/₈") thick wood, painted white; 35 cm x 1 cm (14" x ³/₈") pretty braid

Dressing and decorating the dolls

Using fabric to match the petticoats, make a bodice and skirt for each doll as described on pages 19-21. For the large doll make a large skirt and bodice with long kimono sleeves. Fold excess width of the front bodice into a narrow pleat in the centre, and hemstitch in place. Glue two buttons on top.

For the small doll make a small skirt and bodice with puffed sleeves, and finish the lower edge of the sleeves with a 5 mm (³/₁₆") ruffle.

Large Doll

Cuffs: Finish the lower sleeve edges with 1.5 cm (⁵/₈") cuffs. Cut two 5 cm x 4 cm (2" x 1¹/₂") strips of white fabric. Making 5 mm (³/₁₆") seams, sew the ends of each strip together to form two tubes. Turn the long raw edges under 5 mm (³/₁₆"), fold the strip double, and sew together with small overcast stitches. Sew or glue the cuffs lightly in place around the lower edge of the sleeves.

Apron: From white cotton cut a 9 cm x 11 cm (3¹/₂" x 4¹/₂") apron and a 6 cm x 2 cm (2¹/₂" x ³/₄") waistband. Make 5 mm (³/₁₆") double hems on one long and two short sides of the apron. Gather the raw edge to measure 5 cm (2"). Sew the waistband to the gathered edge with right sides together, raw edges even and centres matched. Turn under 5 mm (³/₁₆") seam on all sides and fold the band double. Using slipstitch, sew the band in place against the back of the apron over the previous stitchline. Cut the 1 cm (³/₈") ribbon in half. Making a narrow turning, sew one piece to each end of the waistband. Fit the apron on the doll, and knot the ties into a bow at centre back.

Crocheted shawl: Crochet abbreviations are on page 12. Make a foundation row of 52ch. Working in dc, dec 1st at each end of every row until 3sts remain. To make a firm edging, cont with one row dc all around shawl, easing the fullness of the foundation row (52ch) to about 43dc. Cont with a decorative edge around the two sides as follows:

1st row: *2ch, miss 1dc, 1dc in next dc*; rep from * – *, turn.
2nd row: *3ch, 1dc in 2ch sp*; rep from * – * to end.
3rd row: Same as second row. Fasten off.

Work chains to make a 10 cm (4") long cord. Fit the shawl on the doll. Lace the cord ends through an opening at each end of the cast-on edge. Knot the cord together and tie into a bow.

'One plain, one purl...' Grandma makes sure that her knowledge of knitting is passed on to the next generation! The sleeves of her dark flowered dress have stylish white cuffs, and she wears a white apron and crocheted shawl. Her charming little granddaughter wears a cream flowered dress, and stands on a decorated wooden base. The dolls can also be made separately, and would make precious keepsakes for someone who loves knitting

Knitting sampler: Using 8-ply red yarn and 2 mm (No 14) knitting needles, cast on 10sts. Work 12 rows rib. Insert one toothpick into the right hand of the doll. Transfer the stitches from the knitting needle onto the toothpick, and wind the yarn end into a small ball. Insert the other toothpick into the left hand. Bend the arms into a realistic position, and glue the ball of yarn lightly to the right-hand lower corner of the apron.

Small doll

For the collar, cut an 18 cm (7") piece of lace. Match the centre of the lace with the centre of the front neck edge of the dress. Sew the lace around the front and sides of the neck edge, forming a square neckline. Cross over the remaining lace at the back, trim surplus and glue the ends onto the raw top edge of the skirt.

Apron: Cut a 6 cm (2½") square of white fabric. Make 5 mm (³/₁₆") wide double hems along three sides. Gather the raw edge to measure 2.5 cm (1"). Sew lace along the hemmed sides to the wrong side of the apron, allowing the lace to show 1 cm (³/₈"). Matching the centres, glue the gathered edge to the front waist over the raw top edge of the skirt. Matching centres, arrange the ribbon ties around the waist, covering the glued edge of the apron and the remaining raw top edge of the skirt. Glue the ribbon in place and knot the ends into a bow at the back. Glue a small white bow onto the hair over each imaginary ear.

Knitting sampler: Work a red knitting sampler in the same way as for the large doll, but cast on only 8 stitches and work only 8 rows rib. Insert the toothpick with knitting in the left hand and the other toothpick in the right hand.

Glue braid over the outer edge of the wooden base. Glue the dolls on top of the base in the centre.

Make 6 small balls of yarn. Glue these inside the basket. Insert two toothpicks through one ball at the top.

7: HERE COMES THE BRIDE!

This romantic decoration would make a beautiful gift for a bride to be. Attended by her two bridesmaids and a flower-girl, the radiant bride is led through an archway of flowers to live happily ever after...!

If you have not much free time, make the bride only, and perhaps one or two attendants. Or, as the happy bride yourself, make for each of your bridesmaids a small doll as a precious keepsake. Dressing the dolls in the actual bridal fabrics would add special sentimental value!

Finished sizes

Bride about 20 cm (8"); bridesmaids and flower-girl about 12 cm (4³/₄"); wooden base 30 cm (12") diameter; flower arch 22 cm high and 18 cm wide (8³/₄" x 7").

Materials

Following the instructions on pages 13-19, make one large and three small basic dolls, with features, hair and petticoats: one large doll with a white taffeta petticoat and basic hairstyle; two small dolls with white-dotted pink petticoats and basic hairstyle; one small doll with white petticoat and rolled plaits over imaginary ears. For dress and petticoats, 30 cm x 115 cm (12" x 45") white moiré taffeta; 20 cm x 115 cm (8" x 45") thin white fabric; 20 cm x 115 cm (8" x 45") thin white-dotted pink fabric

Matching coloured sewing threads

Tracing paper

Pencil and ruler

Clear-drying glue

To decorate the bride:

20 cm x 115 cm (8" x 45") thin tulle veiling; 3 m x 3 mm (3 yds x ¹/₈") white satin ribbon; 50 cm x 1 cm (20" x ³/₈") white taffeta ribbon for the sash; 10 cm x 3 cm (4" x ¹/₄") double-edged ungathered white lace to decorate centre front bodice; 20 cm x 2.5 cm (8" x 1") ungathered white lace for the collar; 60 cm x 1 cm (24" x ³/₈") gathered white lace for the lower dress edge and sleeve edges; eleven 1 cm (³/₈") diameter pearl flower decorations (available per metre); a bouquet made from eight 1 cm (³/₈") diameter white ribbon roses and green leaves with 4 cm (1¹/₂") stems

To decorate two pink bridesmaids:

1.5 m x 2 cm (1¹/₂ yds x ³/₄") white gathered lace for collars and lower dress edges; 30 cm x 1 cm (12" x ³/₈") gathered white lace for the lower sleeve edges; 1 m x 7.5 mm (36" x ¹/₄") taffeta ribbon for sashes; 1 m x 2 mm (36" x ¹/₁₆") white taffeta ribbon for small bows; 80 cm x 7.5 mm (32" x¹/₄") white braid with pale pink and green flowers; 10 pink and 10 white ribbon roses.

For the baskets, small quantities DMC Coton Perle No 8; 1.50 mm crochet hook; tiny pastel coloured flowers and flowerbuds, two small pieces of cardboard

To decorate the white flower-girl:

12 cm x 1.25 cm (5" x ¹/₂") wide ungathered white lace for the collar; 40 cm x 2 cm (16" x ³/₄") white gathered lace for lower dress edge; 50 cm x 5 mm (20" x ³/₁₆") pale pink ribbon for the sash; 50 cm x 2 mm (20" x ¹/₁₆") pink ribbon for small bows; 40 cm x 7.5 mm (16" x ¹/₄") white braid with pale pink and green flowers; 8 pink ribbon roses

For the basket, a small quantity DMC Coton Perle No 8; 1.50 mm crochet hook, tiny pastel coloured flowers and flowerbuds, small piece of cardboard

For the base:

30 cm (12") diameter circle of 1.5 cm (⁵/₈") thick wood, painted white; about 60 cm (24") thick wire (or use three or four 60 cm lengths of thin wire together); 24 pink ribbon roses, 24 white rosebuds, a generous assortment of green leaves and small flowerbuds (all these should be on short wire stems); thin florist's wire and green tape; 1 m x 1 cm (36" x ³/₈") pink taffeta ribbon

Dressing the dolls

For each doll select fabric to match their petticoat, and make a bodice and skirt as described on pages 19-21. For the large doll make a large skirt and bodice with kimono sleeves. For each of the two small dolls with pink petticoats make a small skirt and bodice with kimono sleeves, and finish the lower edge of the sleeves with 1 cm (³/₈") lace and a 1 cm (³/₈") ruffle. For the small doll with white petticoat make a small skirt and bodice with short puffed sleeves, and work a 1 cm (³/₈") ruffle along the lower edge of the sleeves.

Decorating the dolls

The bride

Sew the double-edged lace over the centre front bodice, tuck surplus lace inside the skirt, and glue three pearl flowers over the centre of the lace. Place the sash around the waist, covering the raw top edge of the skirt; glue lightly in place and tie the ends into a bow at the back, forming short loops and long ties. Make 12 small bows using 3 mm (¹/₈") ribbon. Hem the short ends of the lace for the collar and work a row of running stitches along the top edge. Fit the collar on the doll from centre front to centre front. Draw up to fit the neck and fasten off. Glue one small white bow in the centre of the collar.

Sew gathered lace along the inside of the lower sleeve edges. Glue a small white bow over the centre of the sleeve edges, and glue a pearl flower on top of the bow.

Sew lace along the inside of the lower edge of the skirt. Glue 6 small white bows evenly spaced onto the lower edge of the skirt, and glue a pearl flower on top of each bow.

Tie two 15 cm (6") pieces of narrow white ribbon around the bouquet, forming four 7 cm (2³/₄") tie ends. Bend the arms into a realistic position and glue the flower bouquet between the hands. Glue a small bow over the knot of the ties.

Fold the tulle veiling in half twice across its width, to obtain four layers. Work a row of running stitches 1.25 cm (¹/₂") from the top edge (one of the sides without folds) through all four layers. Draw up to fit around the front of the head. Sew three 30 cm (12") pieces of 3 mm (¹/₈") white ribbon together at one end, braiding them to form an 8 cm (3") band. Sew the three pieces together at the other end, and trim excess. Fit the veil over the head and glue lightly in place. Trim the lower edge of the veil if needed. Glue the plaited band over the gathered end of the veiling, 1 cm (³/₈") from the edge, forming a 1 cm (³/₈") veil heading. Glue a small bow over each end of the braided band.

Closeup of the bride's finery

Details of crocheted flower baskets

Bridesmaids and flower-girl

Bridesmaids

Work both dolls the same unless otherwise indicated. Sew gathered lace along the lower edge of the skirt on the right side, and sew flower braid over the top edge of the lace.

For the collar, cut an 18 cm (7") piece of gathered lace. Match the centre of the lace to the centre front neck edge. Sew the lace around the front and sides of the neck edge, forming a square neckline. Cross over the remaining lace at the back, trim surplus, and glue the ends onto the raw top edge of the skirt at the back.

For the sash, cut a length of taffeta ribbon to fit the waist with 1 cm (³/₈") extra. Glue this around the waist to cover the top edge of the skirt and the collar ends. Overlap the ends of the sash at the front of the waist (for one doll on the left side, for the other doll on the right side), and glue a bow with small loops and long ties over the join. Glue a white ribbon rose in the centre of this bow. Glue small white bows over the corners of the collar at the front.

Glue ribbon roses over the hair in a ring, alternating 5 pink and 4 white roses, and glue a small bow between the two pink roses at the back.

Bend the arms into a realistic position, and glue a crocheted flower basket filled with flowers (see method below) over one arm (for one doll over the left arm, for the other over the right arm).

Flower-girl

Decorate the lower edge of the skirt with lace and flower braid as for the bridesmaids.

For the collar, sew the ends of the lace together to form a continuous piece. Work a row of running stitches closely along the straight edge, fit the collar on the doll, draw up and fasten off. Glue a pink bow on the back of the collar at the centre of the neckline. Make a sash in the same way as for the pink dolls, using pink ribbon, and omitting the ribbon rose on the bow. To decorate the head, glue 6 pink ribbon roses into a circle, and add a small pink bow at each side of the head. Bend the arms into a realistic position, and glue a crocheted flower basket filled with flowers (see method below) over the doll's right arm.

Crocheted flower baskets

Crochet abbreviations are on page 12.

Using Perle Coton No 8 and 1.50 mm hook, make 4ch and join with a sl st to form a ring. Cont in rnds, joining each rnd with a sl st.

1st rnd: 8dc around ring.

2nd rnd: 2dc in each dc (16 sts).

3rd rnd: *1dc, 2dc in next dc*; rep from * – * to end (24 sts).

4th rnd: *1dc in each of next 2dc, 2dc in next dc*; rep from * – * to end (32 sts).

5th rnd: *1dc in each of next 3dc, 2dc in next dc*; rep from * – * to end (40 sts).

6th rnd: dc, and work each 4th and 5th dc tog (32 sts).

Work 7 rnds dc.

14th rnd: *2ch, miss 1dc, 1dc in next dc*; rep from * – * to end.

For the handle: Work 30ch, fasten off, and sew the end of the handle to the opposite side of the basket. *Or:* Fasten off, cut 7 cm (2³/₄") of 3 mm (¹/₈") white ribbon, and glue the ends to opposite sides of the basket on the inside.

Insert a 2.5 cm (1") diameter cardboard circle in the baskets for the bridesmaids, and a 2 cm x 3.5 cm (³/₄" x 1³/₈") cardboard oval in the basket for the flower-girl. Arrange the flowers inside the basket, gluing some in place if needed.

White wooden base

Bend the wire into an 18 cm (7") wide arch. Drill two holes in the wooden base, 8 cm (3¹/₄") inside the outer edge and 18 cm (7") apart. Glue the ends of the arch inside the holes and leave to dry thoroughly. Cover about 20 cm (8") of the central curve of the arch with flowers and green leaves. Attach the stems with green florist's tape to the arch, and use glue for some of the flowers and leaves in between. Make two bows with small loops and long ties. Glue one bow to each end of the flower decoration.

Arrange the dolls on the base in the manner suggested by the photograph on page 43. You can either glue them in place or use small pieces of Velcro to make them detachable.

8. 'HAPPY BIRTHDAY'

Finished sizes
Doll 9 cm (3¹/₂"); circular wooden base about 10 cm (4") in diameter.

Materials
A miniature basic doll (see knitting pattern below) with features and basic hairstyle: use a 2 cm (³/₄") diameter foam ball for the head, and 2 cm (³/₄") diameter cardboard and crocheted circles for the base. Omit the fabric circle for the petticoat, using only one layer of 3.5 cm (1¹/₄") gathered lace.

For the dress:
10 cm x 115 cm (4" x 45") fine patterned fabric
30 cm x 5 mm (12" x ³/₁₆") pastel coloured taffeta ribbon
20 cm x 7.5 mm (8" x ¹/₄") pretty flower braid
A small amount of 1.25 cm (¹/₂") white gathered lace
Matching coloured sewing threads
Tracing paper
Pencil and ruler
Clear-drying glue

To decorate:
One 4 cm (1¹/₂") tall bouquet of tiny blue flowers with stems
4 cm x 2.5 cm (1¹/₂" x 1") strong paper for the greeting card (or photocopy the pattern, cut out carefully and use as card) and a tiny flower cut-out
One rectangular and two square shaped pieces of wood or Oasis foam to make gift boxes about 1.5 cm x 2 cm (⁵/₈" x ³/₄"); self-adhesive small patterned wrapping paper and curl sheen ribbon
A 2 cm (³/₄") diameter birthday cake on a 2.25 cm (⁷/₈") high cake stand
For the base, a 10 cm (4") diameter circle of 5 mm (³/₁₆") thick wood, painted white, and 35 cm x 5 mm (14" x ³/₁₆") pretty satin ribbon

Knitting pattern (for the doll)
Assemble and finish the doll as described under General Method on pages 13-19, but use a 2 cm (³/₄") diameter foam ball for the head, 2 cm (³/₄") diameter cardboard and crocheted circles for the base, and make a petticoat from one layer of lace, omitting the fabric circle.

Body
Using white and 3.25 mm (No 10) needles, cast on 20sts.
Work 4 rows rib (2 ridges).
Work 20 rows st st, starting with a knit row. Break off white. Change to pink and 2 mm (No 14) needles to work neck and head.

Neck/Head
Next row: K, and dec 2sts evenly across row (18 sts).
Work 15 rows st st, starting with a purl row.

Shape top of head
Next row: *K2tog*; rep * – * to end of row (9 sts).
Next row: *K2tog*; rep * – * to end of row. Break off yarn, thread end through rem 5 sts, draw up and fasten off.

Arms
Make 2. Using pink and 2 mm (No 14) needles, cast on 4 sts.
1st row: K and inc 1st in each of last 4sts (7 sts).
Work 15 rows st st starting with a purl row.
Cast off.

Dressing and decorating
Make a skirt and bodice (without sleeves) as described on pages 19-21 but adapt the patterns to fit the different measurements of this miniature doll. To do this, draw the outline a few mm within the pattern of the small sized bodice with puffed sleeves, and omit the sleeves. Finish the armholes with gathered lace. For the skirt, use a 15 cm x 6 cm (6" x 2¹/₄") piece of fabric.

Sew flowered braid along the lower edge of the skirt on the right side. Knot the sash around the waist and tie the ends into a bow at the front, making small loops and long ties. Glue a small piece of braid around the head, forming a circle.

Glue the bouquet in the doll's left arm, bending the hand and arm into a realistic position. Photocopy the pattern for the greeting card on page 49 and cut out. Fold the card double and glue the flower cut-out onto the front, below the writing. If making the card yourself, copy the pattern of the card onto strong paper and cut out. Copy the writing with a fine pen. Or cut out sections of small writing on old

Here is an idea to convey the happiest of birthday wishes in a most personal way! This precious keepsake is 9 cm (3½") high, and would also be suitable for a wedding, graduation, anniversary, or birth of a new baby.

The tiny cake decoration is 2 cm (¾") in diameter and 3.5 cm (1¼") high. If such a decoration is difficult to obtain, you may find ways and means of making your own, or you could replace the cake with a small basket filled with flowers. The bouquet in the doll's hand could then be replaced with a bunch of balloons made from lightweight beads or pompoms and wire. Suitable cake decorations, available from cake shops, could also be used greeting cards, and glue in place. Glue the completed card in the doll's hand, bending the arm a little so the card will rest against the body.

To finish

Wrap self-adhesive paper around the small pieces of wood or Oasis to form packages, and tie curl sheen ribbon (cut in half along its width to make it narrower) around the two largest ones. Curl each end of the ribbon by pulling it along the blade of a pair of scissors. Glue satin ribbon around the outer edge of the circular wooden base. Arrange doll, packages and cake on the base (check the photograph for reference) and glue all items in place.

actual size

9: FAIRY GODMOTHERS

Finished sizes

Dolls 20 cm (8"); cane basket 20 cm x 14 cm and 5.5 cm high (8" x 5½", 2¼") embroidered quilt (excluding lace) 12.5 cm x 9 cm (5" x 3½")

Materials

Following the instructions on pages 13-19, make two large basic dolls with features, basic hairstyle and petticoat: one doll has a white taffeta petticoat, the other a mauve taffeta petticoat

30 cm x 115 cm (12" x 45") each white and mauve taffeta fabric

Matching coloured sewing threads

Two 11 cm (4³⁄₈") diameter clear plastic hats, covered with white lace; if these are difficult to obtain you can make hats from 13 cm (5") diameter white crocheted doilies. Soak each doily in a strong starch solution, form a crown by moulding the centre over a round object, and leave to harden

Tracing paper

Pencil and ruler

Clear-drying glue

To decorate the white doll:

1 m x 2 cm (36" x ³⁄₄") white gathered lace

50 cm x 7.5 mm (18" x ¼") white braid with green and mauve flowers

50 cm x 7.5 mm (18" x ¼") white ribbon

Five 1 cm (³⁄₈") pearl flowers

Five 7.5 mm (¼") diameter mauve ribbon roses

Two small bows made from 2 mm (¹⁄₁₆") mauve ribbon

8 cm (3") golden star wand

For the crocheted reticule, small amount of white DMC Coton Perle No 8; 1.50 mm crochet hook; small amount polyester fibre filling; two tiny pearl beads

To decorate the mauve doll:

1 m x 2 cm (36" x ³⁄₄") white gathered lace

50 cm x 7.5 mm (18" x ¼") white braid with pale pink and green flowers

60 cm x 7.5 mm (24" x ¼") pale pink ribbon

Four 7.5 mm (¼") diameter pink ribbon roses

For the umbrella, one 12 cm (5") white pipecleaner covered with white ribbon, with the ribbon ends glued in place

8 cm (3") golden star wand

For the basket, mattress, cushion and quilt:

(*Note:* Materials and instructions are for a 20 cm x 14 cm x 5.5 cm high oval basket (8" x 5½" x 2¼"). Adapt to suit if your basket is a different shape.)

20 cm x 14 cm white oval cane basket, 5.5 cm high (8" x 5½", 2¼")

28 cm (11") diameter white fabric circle

50 cm x 2 cm (18" x ³⁄₄") white gathered lace

50 cm x 4.5 cm (18" x 1¾") white gathered lace with white ribbon insert

For the mattress, 19 cm x 13 cm (7½" x 5¼") white fabric and a small amount of polyester fibre filling

For the cushion, two 8 cm x 11 cm (3" x 4½") pieces white fabric; 40 cm x 1.25 (16" x ½") white gathered lace; small bow made from 2 mm (¹⁄₁₆") pink ribbon; small amount of polyester fibre filling

For the quilt, 20 cm x 15 cm (8" x 6") white count 18 Aida handwork fabric; small quantities stranded embroidery cotton in pale pink, medium pink, dark green and light green; 15 cm x 11 cm (6" x 4½") pink/white checked cotton; 15 cm x 11 cm (6" x 4½") batting; 50 cm x 2 cm (18" x ³⁄₄") white gathered lace

12 cm (5") porcelain baby doll, dressed in a white nightie and bonnet (or as preferred). The doll in the photograph is an heirloom with sentimental value.

Dressing and decorating the dolls

For each doll select fabric to match their petticoat and make a large skirt and bodice with kimono sleeves as described on pages 19-21. Finish the lower edges of the sleeves with lace and a 1 cm (³⁄₈") fabric ruffle.

Both dolls: Sew gathered lace around the lower edge of the skirt on the right side, and sew flower braid over the top edge of the lace.

For the collar, cut 20 cm (8") gathered lace. Match the centre of the lace with the centre of the front neck edge. Sew the lace around the front and sides of the neck edge, forming a square neckline. Cross over the remaining lace at the back, trim surplus, and glue the ends onto the raw top edge of the skirt.

For the sash, glue the ribbon around the waist, covering

Surprise a new mother with this exquisite keepsake! The white basket holds a precious porcelain doll, and is lined and decorated with lace. It has a lace edged cushion and a beautiful embroidered quilt. Two fairy godmothers bestow their gifts on the newborn little one – with their golden wands of course! They have donned their best hats for the occasion

the raw top edge of the skirt and collar ends: for the white doll make a white sash with a bow at the front; for the mauve doll make a pink sash, and make a bow with 8 cm (3") ties.

White doll

Glue two mauve ribbon roses over the bow of the sash, and glue three pearl flowers on the front of the collar along the neck edge. Tie white ribbon around the brim of the hat, making a bow with small loops and long ties at the back. Glue two mauve ribbon roses over the band on the front of the hat, a small mauve bow at each side, and a mauve ribbon rose over the knot of the bow at the back. Glue the hat carefully on the head. Glue the wand in the doll's left hand. Bend the arms into a realistic position and loop the crocheted reticule (see method below) over the right arm.

Crocheted Reticule

See page 12 for crochet abbreviations.

Using Perle Coton No 8 and 1.50 mm hook make 15ch. Join with sl st to form a ring. Cont in rnds, joining each rnd with a sl st.

1st rnd: 6dc around ring.

2nd rnd: 2dc in each dc (12 sts).

3rd rnd: *1dc, 2dc in next dc*; rep from * – * to end (18 sts).

4th rnd: *1dc in each of next 2dc, 2dc in next dc*; rep from

* – * to end (24 sts).

5th rnd: *1dc in each of next 3dc, 2dc in next dc*; rep from * – * to end (30 sts).

6th rnd: *1dc in each of next 4dc, 2dc in next dc*; rep from * – * to end (36 sts).

7th to 17th rnds: Work in dc.

18th rnd: *2ch, miss 2dc, 1dc in next dc*; rep from * – * to end.

19th rnd: *3tr in 2ch sp, sl st in next 2ch sp*; rep from * – * to end.

Work 30ch, break off yarn. Secure the end of the handle to the opposite side of the bag. Fill the bag with polyester fibre filling. Work 55ch to form a cord. Lace the cord through the top edge of the bag, and tie the ends into a bow. Glue a pearl bead to each end.

Tassel: Thread twelve 10 cm (4") lengths of cotton through the centre stitch at the base of the bag, matching the centre of the threads with the centre of the bag. Bunch the threads and tie them together with a short length of cotton (5 mm (³/₁₆") from the base of the bag. Trim the thread ends.

Mauve doll

For the hat, cut two 7 cm (2³/₄") lengths of pink ribbon. Glue one end of each piece each side of the hat to the lower edge of the crown. Bring each piece down over the brim to below the doll's 'chin'. Overlap the ends and glue in place.

Make a pink bow with 1.5 cm (⅝") loops and 8 cm (3") ties. Glue this onto the overlapped ties below the chin, and also to the top edge of the collar. Glue a piece of flower braid around the brim of the hat, covering the ends of the ties at the same time. Glue three pink ribbon roses over the braid at the front of the hat, and one at the back. Glue the wand in the doll's right hand. Make a mauve umbrella as described on page 38. Bend the arms into a realistic position and loop the handle of the umbrella over the left arm.

Basket lining

Turn under 1 cm (⅜") around the white fabric circle. Work a row of running stitches close to the folded edge. Place the circle right side up in the basket with the fold against the top edge, and draw up to fit. Lightly glue the folded edge to the inside of the basket. Glue 2 cm (¾") gathered lace along the top edge on the inside of the basket, with the decorative edge pointing down into the basket. Glue 4.5 cm (1¾") lace with ribbon insert along the top edge on the outside of the basket, placing the ribbon section exactly on the edge.

Mattress and pillow

Use 1 cm (⅜") seams throughout. Sew the pieces for the mattress right sides together, leaving a small opening for turning: round the corners, shaping the mattress into an oval to fit the basket. Cut away the seam corners and clip the seam curves. Turn the mattress right side out. Fill with polyester fibre filling, and sew the opening closed. Make the pillow the same way but with square corners. Sew lace around the outer edge of the pillow, and glue a small pink bow in one corner.

Quilt

First embroider a grid of squares over the centre of the Aida fabric, each square being 15 Aida fabric squares wide and 15 long. Using 1 strand of pale pink embroidery cotton, work the squares with rows of back stitch one Aida fabric square long. Work a total of 5 horizontal rows and 7 vertical rows to obtain a grid of 6 squares horizontally, and 4 squares vertically.

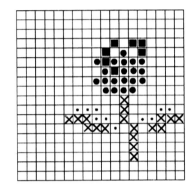

■ pale pink

● medium pink

✕ dark green

· light green

Embroidery graph for quilt

Closeup of the new baby

Detail of crocheted reticule

52

Following the graph and colour key, embroider a rosebud motif in the centre of alternate squares (see photograph). Work in cross-stitch over one Aida fabric square, using two strands of embroidery cotton. When completed, cut the embroidered piece 1 cm (³/₈") outside the pink backstitches. Cut the backing and wadding the same size. Place the front and back with right sides together, and the wadding on top. Sew together just outside the pink embroidered lines, leaving a small opening in the centre of one side for turning. Trim the seams and cut away the seam corners diagonally. Turn the quilt right side out, and sew the opening closed. Sew gathered lace around the quilt on the back.

To finish

Put the mattress and pillow inside the lined basket. Lay the doll in the basket and arrange the quilt on top. Position a fairy godmother at each side of the basket. (If you prefer you can glue them all to a white wooden base, or use Velcro strips to keep them in place.)

10: TEATIME IN THE NURSERY

Finished sizes

Mother 20 cm (8"); nanny 18 cm (7"); toddler with apron 14 cm (5½"); three sitting toddlers 12 cm (4¾"); baby 7 cm (2¾")

Materials

Mother: 1 large basic doll (see page 13) with features, hair with bun on top of head, and blue flowered petticoat

Nanny: 1 large basic doll 2 cm (¾") shorter than usual (see page 13 – when knitting the doll, omit about 8 rows from the body) with features, basic hairstyle, and blue/white striped petticoat

Girl with apron: 1 small basic doll 2 cm (¾") taller than usual (see page 14 – when knitting the doll, add about 8 rows to the body) with features, one plait at the back tied with a bow made from 7.5 mm (¼") white ribbon, and pink dotted petticoat

Dolls in chairs: 2 small dolls with legs (see page 15), with bloomers, features and plait over head

Doll with koala: 1 small doll with legs, with a shorter body and arms than usual (see page 15 – when knitting the doll, omit 4 rows from the body and 2 from the arms), features, basic hairstyle and short bloomers

Baby: 1 basic baby doll (see pattern on page 57), with features, but no hair or petticoat

25 cm x 115 cm (10" x 45") blue fabric with very pale blue flowers; 20 cm x 115 cm (8" x 45") white-dotted pink fabric; 20 cm x 115 cm ((8" x 45") white-dotted blue fabric; 20 cm x 115 cm (8" x 45") narrow blue/white striped fabric; 20 cm x 115 cm (8" x 45") white fabric; 15 cm x 20 cm (6" x 8") cream fabric

Matching coloured sewing threads

Tracing paper

Pencil and ruler

Clear-drying glue

To decorate the mother doll:

45 cm x 2 cm (18" x ¾") ungathered white lace; 80 cm x 3 mm (32" x ⅛") pale pink ribbon; 7 cm x 3 cm (2¾" x 1¼") double-edged white ungathered lace for centre front bodice; 15 cm x 1.75 cm (6" x ⅝") ungathered white lace for collar; 8 small flat rhinestones; 40 cm x 1 cm (16" x ⅜") pale blue ribbon for the sash; nine 7.5 mm

(¼") diameter blue ribbon roses for the head; small hand-bag (either a 3.5 cm (1½")beaded necklace pendant or the small crocheted reticule from page 51).

To decorate the nanny:

30 cm x 1.5 cm (12" x ⅝") white gathered lace for the cap; 1 small mother-of-pearl button; 30 cm x 7.5 mm (12" x ¼") white ribbon for apron-skirt ties

To decorate the four toddlers and baby doll:

For toddler with apron:

40 cm x 1 cm (16" x ⅜") ungathered lace for the apron; 15 cm x 7.5 mm (6" x ¼") white ribbon and 7 pink and 7 white 7.5 mm (¼") diameter ribbon roses for hairband; 25 cm x 7.5 mm (10" x ¼") white ribbon for apron-skirt ties; 3.5 cm (1½") flocked blue horse

For pink toddler in chair:

30 cm x 7.5 mm (12" x ¼") white braid with pale pink and green flowers; 12 cm x 2 cm (5" x ¾") white gathered lace for the collar; 20 cm x 3 mm (8" x ⅛") pink ribbon for small bows; 25 cm x 7.5 mm (10" x ¼") pink ribbon for the sash; 2 small flat rhinestones; 3 cm (1¼") white flocked bear; white wooden chair 11 cm (4½") high with 4 cm (1½") legs and a 5 cm (2") square seat: if such chairs (also needed for the pink doll) are difficult to obtain, make them yourself, or use similar sized dolls' house furniture

For blue toddler in chair:

40 cm x 1 cm (16" x ⅜") pretty flowered ribbon; 12 cm x 2 cm (5" x ¾") white gathered lace for the collar; 10 cm x 1 cm (4" x ⅜") ungathered lace for the sleeve edges; 3 small flat rhinestones; four 7.5 mm (¼") diameter blue ribbon roses for the head; 30 cm x 3 mm (12" x ⅛") white ribbon for small bows; 4 tiny pastel flowers tied to form a 4 cm (1½") bouquet; 3 cm (1¼") brown flocked bear; white wooden chair 16 cm (6¼") high, with 4 cm (1½") legs and a seat 7 cm by 5.5 cm (2¾" x 2¼")

For pink toddler with koala:

30 cm x 2 cm (12" x ¾") white gathered lace, 25 cm x 7.5 mm (10" x ¼") white braid with pale pink and green

Who could resist this idyllic scene? The table is laid in the nursery. Everyone waits for mother to pour the milk and put out the biscuits. The toddlers all wear their best party dresses, because they are celebrating the arrival of a new little sibling into the nursery! Dear old nanny is in charge, dressed in her nanny uniform of course! Each child cuddles a toy they received as a special treat on this happy day. The complete scene, or individual dolls, would make a unique gift to welcome a new baby, or a special surprise for someone dear

Nanny and the new baby

Where I go, my horse goes too

Three of the new baby's four sisters

flowers; 30 cm x 3 mm (12" x ⅛") pink ribbon for sash and small bows; 3 cm (1¼") grey koala; 9 cm (3½") diameter circle of 1 cm (⅜") thick wood, painted white

For the baby doll:
20 cm x 2 cm (8" x ¾") white gathered lace and 15 cm x 3 mm (6" x ⅛") white ribbon for the bonnet; 10 cm x 1 cm (4" x ⅜") white gathered lace for the bonnet; 10 cm x 1 cm (4" x ⅜") white gathered lace for the lower sleeve edges; 8 cm x 4 cm (3" x 1½") painted wooden cradle with rockers, with a cushion and blanket: the cradle in the photograph was bought from a folk-art supply shop, and the lace-edged cushion and blanket (decorated with a tiny wooden bluebird and embroidered with French knots and detached chain stitch) made to fit the cradle

For table with embroidered tablecloth:
White wooden table, 11.5 cm x 6.5 cm, about 5.5 cm high or 4½" x 2½", 2¼" (if your table is a different size, adapt the measurements of the tablecloth to suit); for the table-cloth 25 cm x 20 cm (10" x 8") count 14 Aida handwork fabric; small quantities stranded embroidery cottons in pale rose, rose and pale green; 70 cm x 1 cm (28" x ⅜") ungathered white lace; small tapestry needle; miniature porcelain teaset

Dressing the dolls

Refer to pages 19-21. For the *mother*, *nanny* and *doll with apron*, select fabric to match their petticoats. For the *mother* make a large skirt and bodice with kimono sleeves, with a 7.5 mm (¼") ruffle on the lower sleeve edges. For the *nanny* make a large skirt and bodice with kimono sleeves, adjusting the length of the skirt to the shorter body. For the *doll with apron* make a small skirt and bodice with puffed sleeves, with a 1 cm (⅜") ruffle on the lower sleeve edges, adjusting the length of the skirt to the longer body.

For the *pink doll in chair* use white-dotted pink fabric, and make a small skirt and bodice with puffed sleeves and a 1 cm (⅜") ruffle on the lower sleeve edges. For the *blue doll in chair* use white-dotted blue fabric, and make a small skirt and bodice with kimono sleeves. For the *pink doll with koala* use white-dotted pink fabric, omitting the skirt and making a dress from the small bodice with kimono sleeves by adding extra length to the lower edge. Finish the lower edge of the sleeves with lace and a 1 cm (⅜") fabric ruffle. For the *baby doll* use cream fabric and the pattern for the nightdress on page 58. Work the nightdress in the same way as the bodice with kimono sleeves, and finish the lower edge of the sleeves with lace and a 1 cm (⅜") fabric ruffle.

Decorating the dolls

Mother

Sew 2 cm (¾") lace along the lower edge of the skirt on the right side. Glue 3 mm (⅛") pink ribbon over the top edge of the lace. Sew double-edged lace down the centre of the front bodice, from neck edge to waist, tucking the raw edge of the lace inside the skirt. For the collar, make a narrow hem on both short ends of the lace. Work a row of running stitches along the straight edge. Fit the collar on the doll from centre front to centre front, draw up to fit the neck and fasten off. Glue a small pink bow between the two collar ends.

Tie the ribbon for the sash around the waist, forming a bow at the back. Glue 4 rhinestones over the centre of the

56

double-edged lace on the bodice, and two rhinestones over the centre of each lower sleeve edge. Glue ribbon roses on the front and sides of the head, and two small bows on each side of the bun. Bend the arms and place the handle of the bag around the doll's right arm.

Nanny

Using white cotton and ribbon, work an apron following the instructions on page 68, and fit to the doll.

Cuffs: From white cotton cut a 6 cm x 4 cm (2¼" x 1½") strip for each cuff. Using a 5 mm (³/₁₆") seam, sew the short ends of each strip together to form a continuous piece. Fold the strip in half lengthwise, with wrong sides together, making it 2 cm (¾") wide. Turn both long raw sides 5 mm (³/₁₆") inwards, and work a row of running stitches through all four layers, close to the edge. Fit the cuff over the sleeve (the gathered edge forms the lower edge), gather up to fit the wrist, and fasten off.

Collar: From white fabric, cut four collar shapes from the pattern on page 58. Using a narrow seam, sew the pieces together in pairs, leaving small openings for turning. Clip all seam curves and turn right side out. Sew each collar section along the neck edge from centre front to centre back. Glue a small button between the two collar sections at the front.

Cap: From white fabric cut an 11 cm (4½") diameter circle. Turn edges 1 cm (³/₈") under, and sew lace along the outer edge on the wrong side. Make a row of running stitches 1 cm (³/₈") inside the outer fabric edge. Fit the cap on the doll, draw up and fasten off. Glue lightly in place.

Toddler with apron

Using white fabric and ribbon, work an apron following the pattern on page 68, adjusting the measurements to the smaller size, and decorate the outer edges of the skirt and bib with lace.

For the headband, use the 15 cm (6") white ribbon, and glue 7 pink and 7 white ribbon roses in the centre, alternating the colours. Glue into a circle over the head, cutting away excess ribbon. Bend the arms and place the blue horse in the doll's left arm. You might like to link the toddler's right arm through the mother's left arm.

Pink toddler in chair

Sew braid along the lower edge of the skirt on the right side, 1 cm (³/₈") inside the lower edge. Hem the two short sides of the collar, and work running stitches along the straight edge. Fit the collar on the doll from centre back to centre back, draw up and fasten off.

Tie ribbon for the sash around the waist, forming long ties at the front. Glue two rhinestones over the collar at the front. Glue small pink bows to the hair at each end of the plait. Place the white bear in the left arm. Bend the legs,

and place the doll in the chair. Glue lightly in place.

Blue toddler in chair

Work this the same way as for the pink doll above, but using pretty ribbon to decorate the lower edge of the dress, and for the sash (making a sash without a bow, overlapping the ends at the back); glue three rhinestones over the collar; finish the lower edge of the sleeves with lace; glue a blue bow and two blue ribbon roses to the hair at each end of the plait; glue the bouquet in the right hand and the brown bear in the left arm.

Pink toddler with koala

Sew lace along the lower edge of dress on the right side, and sew braid over the top edge of the lace. Glue braid to the head in a circle. Bend the arms, and glue the koala against the two hands at the front. Glue a pink bow to each 'foot'. Bend the legs, and glue the doll to the centre of the wooden base.

To make the toy building block, use six pieces of plastic canvas, each 6 meshes long and 7 meshes wide, and scraps of 8-ply yarns in six different pastel colours. Work a straight stitch or cross-stitch over each mesh, filling in the entire background of each piece. Using 8-ply white yarn, join the edges of the pieces with overcast stitches to form a cube. Glue the cube to the base in front of the doll.

Baby doll pattern

Follow the knitting pattern below for the basic doll, assembling and finishing it following the instructions on page 15. Use a 2 cm (¾") diameter foam ball, and 2 cm (¾") diameter cardboard and crocheted circles; omit the hair and petticoat and work only the features.

Body and head

Using pink and 2 mm (No 14) needles, cast on 16sts.
Work 4 rows rib (2 ridges).
Work 28 rows st st, starting with a knit row.
Next row: K2 tog, rep to end of row (8 sts).
Next row: K2 tog, rep to end of row (4 sts). Break off yarn, thread yarn end through rem sts, draw up and fasten off.

Arms

Make 2. Using pink and 2 mm (No 14) needles, cast on 4 sts.
1st row: K, and inc 1st in each st (8sts).
Work 3 rows rib (2 ridges).
Work 12 rows st st, starting with a knit row. Cast off and assemble.

Decorating the baby doll

Sew lace around the lower sleeve edges of the nightie on the inside. Trace the bonnet pattern, and cut out from white fabric. Using a narrow seam, sew the two sides together as indicated. Make a narrow hem all around, and sew gathered lace along the front. Cut the 3 mm (¹/₈") ribbon in half, and sew a piece to each end for ties. Fit the bonnet on

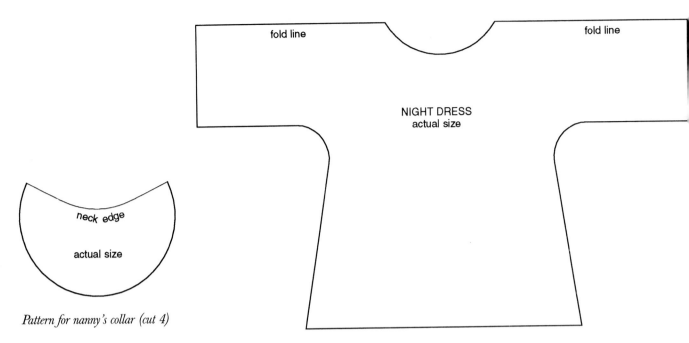

Pattern for nanny's collar (cut 4)

Pattern for baby's night dress, including 6 mm (¹/₄ ") seam allowances

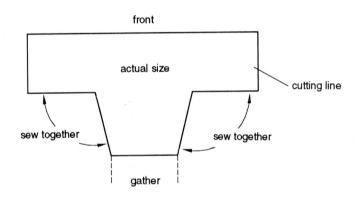

Pattern for baby's bonnet

the doll, and tie a small bow below the chin. Place the doll in the cradle.

Tablecloth

Following the graph, embroider the border on the Aida fabric, working in cross-stitch over one Aida square, using two strands of embroidery cotton. When completed, cut the Aida fabric 1.5 cm (⁵/₈") outside the embroidered frame. Press the edges 5 mm (³/₁₆") under and sew lightly in place. Sew lace around the tablecloth on the inside. Place the cloth over the table: to keep the corners in place, make a few small stitches with white sewing thread. Place (or glue) the tea-service on top of the table.

To finish

Arrange the dolls into a harmonious scene, using the photograph on page 55 as a guide. You might prefer to glue the scene to a decorated wooden base.

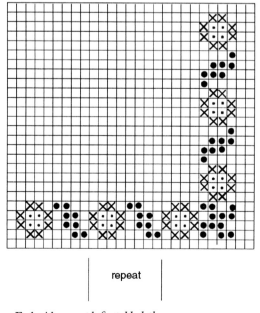

● pale green
✕ rose
· pale rose

Embroidery graph for tablecloth

11: TREETOP ANGELS

These two festive ornaments are 17 cm (6 ³/₄") high. Although both angels have been worked from the same pattern, they are distinct individuals. Make one for the tree-top, or place an angel amid fragrant Christmas greenery for a special window setting or table-top centrepiece

Finished size
17 cm (6³/₄")

Materials
For each angel make a medium basic doll with features, basic hairstyle, and petticoat made from dress fabric, following the instructions on pages 14-19. (*Note:* When knitting the doll, add 8 more rows to the white body to make the doll about 2 cm (³/₄") taller and more elegant)

25 cm x 115 cm (10" x 45") thin fabric, either pale green with small white flowers, or white self-flowered print

Matching coloured sewing threads

Tracing paper

Pencil and ruler

Clear-drying glue

To decorate the white angel:

For the dress: 1 m x 1 cm (36" x ³/₈") gold braid; 1 m x 3 mm (36" x ¹/₈") gold-edged cream satin ribbon

For the head: 10 cm x 1 cm (4" x ³/₈") gold braid

For the wreath, a 5 cm (2") diameter (outer edge) green wreath; 4 small gold Christmas balls; 40 cm x 3 mm (16" x ¹/₈") red ribbon

For the wings, 10 cm (4") square double-sided gold cardboard

To decorate the green angel:

For the dress, 50 cm x 7.5 mm (20" x ¹/₄") gold ribbon; 30 cm x 3 mm (12" x ¹/₈") gold-edged cream satin ribbon; 40 cm x 2 cm (6" x ³/₄") gathered white lace

For the head, 5 small gold Christmas balls

For decorations in hands, 3 cm (1¹/₄") golden star laced to a small piece of gold cord; 8 cm (3") white birthday-cake candle in holder

For the wings, 10 cm (4") square double-sided gold cardboard

Dressing and decorating
Use fabric to match the petticoat, and make a medium sized bodice and skirt, cutting the skirt 2 cm (³/₄") longer, as described on pages 19-21. For the green angel, work the bodice with kimono sleeves. For the white angel, work the bodice with long puffed sleeves, making a narrow ruffle on the lower edge.

White angel
Sew gold braid to the bottom of the skirt on the right side, about 1 cm (³/₈") up from the lower edge. Glue gold-edged ribbon over the sewn top edge of the braid. Decorate the lower edge of the sleeves in the same way, with the gold edge of the ribbon edging the sleeve. Cut 20 cm (8") gold braid, match the centre with the centre front neck, and sew it around the front and sides of the neck edge, forming a square neckline. Cross over the remaining braid at the back, trim surplus, and glue the ends onto the raw top edge of skirt at the back. For the sash, glue gold-edged cream satin ribbon around the waist, covering the raw top edge of the skirt and braid ends. Knot the sash at the back, forming 5

cm (2") ties. To make a crown, form a ring of gold braid to fit the head, and glue in place.

Trace the wing pattern onto tracing paper, copy on gold cardboard and cut out. Fold the wings outwards on the dotted lined. Glue the centre of the wings to the centre of the back of the angel.

Wind red ribbon around the wreath, and decorate with gold balls glued on top. Tie a red bow with small loops and 6 cm (2¹/₄") ends and glue to the bottom of the wreath. Bend the angel's arms so the hands are pointing towards each other and glue the back of the wreath to the hands.

Green angel
For the collar, cut 20 cm (8") gathered lace. Match the centre of the lace with the centre front neck and sew it around the front and sides of the neck edge to form a square neckline. Cross over the remaining lace at the back, trim surplus, and glue the ends onto the raw top edge of the skirt. Glue a piece of gold-edged cream ribbon over the sewn edge of the lace, following the neckline and also the crossing at the back. For the sash, glue gold ribbon around the waist, covering the raw top edge of the skirt and lace and ribbon ends. Knot the ends of the sash at the front, making a bow with 1.5 cm (⁵/₈") loops and 10 cm (4") ends. Sew white lace to the inside of the lower sleeve edges, and glue gold-edged cream ribbon around the sleeves, about 5 mm (³/₁₆") up from the lower edge.

Glue the gold balls side by side over the front of the head, forming a crown. Bend the arms and hands into a realistic position. Loop the cord of the golden star around the right hand, and glue in place. Insert the pointed base of the candle holder through the left hand. Make wings as for the white angel.

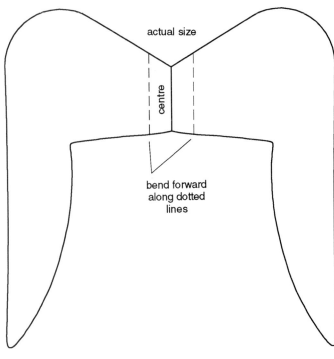

actual size

centre

bend forward along dotted lines

Pattern for angel's wings

12: THE SOUNDS OF MUSIC

Finished sizes
Tree about 30 cm (12") high, dolls 16 cm and 13.5 cm (6¼" and 5¼").

Materials
Following the instructions on pages 14-19, make one medium and one small basic doll, each with petticoat, features, and plait over head hairstyle

For dresses/petticoats, 20 cm x 115 cm (8" x 45") thin red Christmas fabric

For apron and blouse, 10 cm x 115 cm (4" x 45") thin white fabric, 24 cm x 7.5 cm (9¼" x ¼") white taffeta ribbon for apron ties

For apron, collars and sleeve edges, 1 m x 1.25 cm (36" x ½") ungathered white lace
Matching coloured sewing threads
Tracing paper
Pencil and ruler
Clear-drying glue

To decorate the dolls:
3 small bows made from 3 mm (⅛") ribbon (1 black, 2 red)
2 x 1 cm (⅜") diameter red ribbon roses
6.5 cm (2½") wooden or golden violin
7 cm (2¾") toothpick
6 cm (2¼") Christmas tree
2.5 cm (1") brown flocked bear
2 circular wooden bases, 10 cm and 11 cm in diameter (4" and 4¼") painted white
80 cm x 1 cm (32" x ⅜") white satin ribbon

31 cm (12¼") Christmas tree; 20 x 1 cm (⅜") diameter golden bells; 2.5 m x 5 mm (2½ yd x ³/₁₆") red ribbon; narrow silver tinsel; 3 cm (1¼") golden star

Dressing and decorating
Using fabric to match petticoats, make bodices and skirts as described on pages 19-21. For the medium doll make a medium sized red skirt and white bodice with puffed sleeves, and finish the lower edge of the sleeves with a narrow ruffle. For the small doll make a small sized red skirt and red bodice with kimono sleeves, and finish the lower edge of the sleeves with lace and a 3 mm (⅛") ruffle.

Large doll
For the skirt band, cut a 12 cm x 2 cm (4¾" x ¾") strip red fabric. Press under 5 mm (³/₁₆") on both long sides and one short side. Glue the band over the raw top edge of the skirt, matching the centre with the centre front, and overlap the ends at centre back.

For the collar, use 14 cm (5½") lace, sewing the ends together to form a continuous piece. Work a row of running stitches along the straight edge. Fit the collar on the doll, draw up and fasten off. Decorate the front of the collar with a black bow.

Glue a red rose on the hair over each imaginary ear. Bend the arms into a realistic position. Glue one end of the violin in the left hand and the other end below the left cheek. Glue the toothpick in the right hand.

Glue white satin ribbon around the outer edge of the 11 cm (4¼") diameter wooden base. Glue the doll to the centre.

Small doll
For the apron, cut an 8.5 cm x 6 cm piece (3½" x 2¼") from white fabric. Hem one long and two short sides with a 5 mm (³/₁₆") double hem. Sew lace around the hemmed edges, on the inside, allowing the lace to show about 7.5 mm (¼"). Gather the raw edge to measure 3 cm (1¼"). Matching the centres, glue this edge to the waist at the front, over the raw top edge of the skirt. Matching the centre of the ribbon with the centre of the apron, arrange the ribbon ties around the waist, covering the glued edge of the apron and remaining top edge of the skirt. Glue the ribbon in place, and knot the ends into a bow at the back.

For the collar, use 13 cm (5") white lace and work it as described for the larger doll. Glue a red bow on the hair over each imaginary ear. Glue the bear in the left arm, and the tree in the right arm, bending the arms into a realistic position.

Glue ribbon around the outer edge of the 10 cm (4") diameter wooden base. Glue the doll in the centre.

Christmas tree
Lace each bell onto a 12 cm (5") length of 5 mm (³/₁₆") red ribbon, and tie the ribbon into a bow. Decorate the tree with the bells, gluing the backs of the bows to the tips of the branches. Glue the star to the top branch.

Decorate the tree with silver tinsel. Arrange the dolls under the tree.

The Sounds of Music: A Christmas tree and the sweet sounds of violin music! This appealing duo, dressed in festive red and pristine white, symbolises the spirit of Christmas in a most delightful way. Instructions appear on page 61

13: ANGEL CONCERT

Finished sizes
Angels 12 cm (5"); base 18 cm x 6 cm (7" x 2¼")

Materials
For three knitted angels:
1 x 50g ball white 4-ply yarn
1 x 25g ball pale pink 4-ply yarn
2 mm (No 14) knitting needles
Small amount of 4-ply woollen yarn in desired colour for the hair
Small quantity DMC stranded embroidery cottons in medium brown and pink for the features
6 x 12 cm (5") white pipecleaners
3 x 2.25 cm (1") diameter white foam balls
Polyester fibre filling
Clear-drying glue

To decorate the angels:
75 cm x 7.5 mm (30" x ¼") ribbon or cord for sashes (makes 3)
30 cm x 7.5 mm (12" x ¼") gold braid and 15 cm (6") pretty flowered braid for head decorations
1.5 cm (⅝") diameter golden bell on a short length of thin gold thread; golden trumpet and violin, each 4.5 cm (1½") long (available as Christmas tree decorations); 6 cm (2¼") toothpick coloured brown with a felt pen
10 cm (4") gold cord for angel with bell

2 x 9 cm (3½") outer diameter Christmas candle/bottle rings made from green leaves, white flowers and red berries (or make your own rings using florist's wire and small silk flowers and leaves)
18 cm x 6 cm (7" x 2½") of 5 mm (³⁄₁₆") thick wood, painted white

Angel pattern
This knitting pattern for a 12 cm (5") angel is used for each of the three angels. Assemble and finish the angels as described on pages 13-19, but omit the petticoat and the cardboard and crocheted circles at the base. Instead, leave a short section of the lower back seam of the body open for easy filling. When the foam ball and fibre filling have been

inserted, close the rest of the seam, and form a flat base by pushing the cast-on edge in slightly. Give each angel a basic hairstyle, brown eyes and a pink mouth.

Body and head
Using white and 2 mm (No 14) needles, cast on 12sts.
1st row: K, and inc 1st in each st (24 sts).
Work 25 rows st st, starting with a purl row. Break off white and change to pink to work neck and head.
Next row: K, and dec 2sts evenly across row (22 sts).
Work 15 rows st st, starting with a purl row.
Next row: K2tog; rep to end of row (11 sts).
Next row: K2tog; rep to end of row (6 sts).
Break off yarn. Thread yarn end through remaining sts, draw up and fasten off.

Arms
Work 2. Using pink and 2 mm (No 14) needles, cast on 4sts.
1st row: K, and inc 1st in each st (8 sts).
Work 5 rows st st, starting with a purl row. Change to white.
Work 14 rows st st, starting with a knit row. Cast off.

Wings
Using white and 2 mm (No 14) needles, cast on 30 sts.
Knit all rows (rib).
Knit 2sts tog at beg and end of every row, until 2sts rem on needle. Cast off, and use end of yarn to work small running stitches through the centre of the wing. Draw up tightly to shape the wing and fasten off. Sew or glue the centre of the wing to the back of the angel.

Decorating

Angel with bell
Glue a piece of flowered braid over the head in a circle. Cut away excess. Tie a piece of blue ribbon around the waist to form a sash with long ties, and glue lightly in place. Glue a small section of the flower braid over the knot of the sash. Bend the arms, and sew the ends of the hands together, with the hanging thread of the bell glued in between. Glue a bow made from gold cord to the hands.

Join in the spirit of the festive season with this delightful musical trio. Their heavenly music brings peace and goodwill ... and a smile to anyone's face! This original Christmas decoration is very easy to work, and the costs of materials are minimal

Angel with violin

Glue a small piece of gold braid over the head, forming a circle. Tie a piece of ribbon around the waist to form a sash with long ties, and glue in place. Glue one end of the violin in the left hand, and the other end below the left cheek, bending the arm into a realistic position. Carefully glue the brown toothpick in the right hand, and bend the arm into a realistic position.

Angel with trumpet

Glue a small piece of gold braid around the head. Cut away excess. Glue the trumpet between the hands with the mouthpiece directly below the mouth, bending the arms into a realistic position. Tie a piece of ribbon around the waist to form a sash with long ties, and glue in place.

Optional: Use cord instead of ribbon for the sash. Twirling in one direction, twist together four 50 cm (20") pieces white yarn and 50 cm (20") gold cord. Keeping the twisted strand taut, thread it through a heavy object, such as the handle of a pair of scissors, till it doubles. Holding both ends together, allow the scissors to hang downwards and twirl to form a cord. Knot the ends. Cut the cord free from the scissors and trim the yarn ends even. Tie around the angel's waist.

To finish

Glue the angel with bell in the centre of the wooden base. Stand the other angels inside a Christmas candle/bottle decoration and position them on the wooden base, as in the photographs. Glue to base.

14: MR AND MRS SANTA

MR SANTA

Finished size
20 cm (8")

Materials
30g 8-ply red yarn
Small quantities 8-ply yarn in white and pink
Scraps of black yarn for eyes
3.25 mm (No 10) knitting needles
2.5 cm crochet hook
Large-eyed tapestry needle
Clear-drying glue
4 cm (1¹/₂") diameter white foam ball
Polyester fibre filling
5.5 cm (2¹/₈") diameter circle of strong cardboard
5.5 cm (2¹/₈") crocheted circle
1 x 1.5 cm (⁵/₈") diameter and 4 x 6 mm (¹/₄") diameter white pompoms
15 cm x 1.75 cm (6" x ⁵/₈") metallic gold ribbon for the sash

For Santa's bag:
8 cm x 20 cm (3" x 8") cotton Christmas fabric; 30 cm x 7.5 mm (12" x ¹/₄") metallic gold ribbon, cut in two; 4 cm (1¹/₂") piece of Christmas greenery; 2.5 cm (1") flocked brown teddy bear with 10 cm (4") thin gold cord tied around its neck

For decoration in arm, 4 x 7 cm (2³/₄") sprigs of fine Christmas greenery; 2 cm (³/₄") red toadstool
For decoration in hand, 5 cm (2") golden trumpet and small bow made from 2 mm (¹/₁₆") red ribbon
For hat decoration, 2 x 3 cm (1¹/₄") holly leaves with red berries and small red bow made from 2 mm (¹/₁₆") red ribbon

Pattern for Mr Santa
Follow the knitting pattern below to make Mr Santa. Assemble and finish the doll as described on pages 13-19, but omit petticoat and hair, and work eyes in black and mouth in red, using knitting yarns. Sew white seams with white yarn and red seams with red yarn.

Body/head
Using white and 3.25 mm (No 10) needles, cast on 32sts.
Work 4 rows rib (2 ridges).
Break off white and change to red.
Work 40 rows st st, starting with a knit row.
Break off red and change to pink for the head.
1st row: K, and dec 3sts evenly across row (29 sts).
Work 15 rows st st, starting with a purl row.
Next row: K2tog; rep to end of row, K1 (16 sts).
Next row: K2tog; rep to end of row, K1 (8 sts).
Break off yarn, thread yarn end through rem sts, draw up and fasten off.

Arms
Make 2. Using white and 3.25 mm (No 10) needles, cast on 5 sts.
1st row: K, and inc 1st in each st (10 sts).
Work 5 rows rib (3 ridges). Break off white and change to red.
Work 20 rows st st, starting with a knit row. Cast off.

Crocheted circle
Work a 5.5 cm (2¹/₈") diameter white circle following the instructions on page 15.

Beard
Using white and 3.25 mm (No 10) needles, cast on 30 sts. Knit all rows (rib), and knit 2sts tog at beg and end of every row until 2sts rem on needle. Cast off.

Knitted hat
Using white and 3.25 mm (No 10) needles, cast on 30sts.
Work 4 rows rib (2 ridges). Break off white and change to red.
5th and 6th rows: st st.
7th row: K2tog at beg and end of row.
8th row: P.
Rep last 2 rows until there are no more sts left on needle. Close centre back seam.

Decorating Mr Santa
Glue the large white pompom to the pointed end of the hat. Glue the hat over the doll's head. Bring the pointed end

Mr Santa is fully knitted, and carries a bag sewn from special Christmas fabric on his back.

over sideways, towards the right side of the face, and glue the crease lightly in place. Glue holly leaves and bow onto the left side of the hat. Sew the cast-on edge of the beard around the face. Glue the wide gold band around the waist, overlapping the ends at the back of the body. Glue 4 pompoms evenly spaced to the front of the body (one on the sash). Glue Christmas greenery and toadstool in the left arm, and the trumpet with small red bow in the left hand. Bend the arms into a realistic position and glue or sew each hand lightly in place against the body.

Santa's bag
Work a narrow hem on both short sides of the Christmas fabric. Fold the fabric double with right sides together, and sew the sides closed. Clip the seam corners, turn the bag right side out, and fill with polyester fibre filling. Insert the piece of Christmas greenery into the bag, allowing it to stick out at the top. Tie one of the pieces of 7.5 mm ($^1/_4$") metallic gold ribbon around the top of the bag, and tie the ends into a bow. Sew the bear onto the outside of the bag, just below the gold bow, stitching through the gold cord around its neck. Fold the second piece of gold ribbon into a loop, overlap the ends slightly and glue this section against the back of the bag. Glue the bag behind the right shoulder on the doll's back, and arrange the gold loop around the right arm.

MRS SANTA

Finished size
20 cm (8")

Materials
One large basic doll (see page 13) with features, a red petticoat, and only a small section of the front face/head covered with grey hair (because the doll wears a hat). Follow the style for hair parted in the middle (see page 18 and the photograph of Mrs Santa opposite).

For the dress/petticoat, 25 cm x 115 cm (10" x 45") thin red fabric

For the apron, thin white fabric: apron skirt 12 cm x 10 cm (5" x 4"); bib 7 cm x 4 cm ($2^3/_4$" x $1^1/_2$"); waistband 8 cm x 3 cm (3" x $1^1/_4$"); 40 cm x 1 cm (16" x $^3/_8$") white ribbon for waist-ties (cut in 2); 24 cm x 1 cm (10" x $^3/_8$") ribbon for bib-ties (cut in 2)

Matching coloured sewing threads

Tracing paper

Pencil and ruler

Clear-drying glue

One small mother-of-pearl button

To decorate the lower edge of the dress, 45 cm x 2 cm (18" x $^3/_4$") gathered Christmas lace

For the collar and cuffs, about 40 cm x 3 cm (16" x $1^1/_4$") white broder cotton lace

For the hat, small quantities of red and white 8-ply yarn; one 1.5 cm ($^5/_8$") diameter white pompom; two 3 cm

($1^1/_4$") holly leaves with red berries; small bow made from 3 mm ($^1/_8$") red ribbon

3 x 6 cm ($2^1/_2$") pieces of fine Christmas greenery

One 4 cm ($1^1/_2$") oval straw basket, and one 3 cm ($1^1/_4$") white flocked teddy bear holding three tiny balloons (or use any preferred small ornament)

One 7 cm ($9^3/_4$") diameter Christmas wreath with greenery 2 cm ($^3/_4$") wide; the wreath in the photograph is a shop-bought candle/bottle decoration. To make your own, twist wire and Christmas green into a circle and glue on small berries and gumnuts to decorate.

For glasses, about 14 cm ($5^1/_2$") fine gold wire

Dressing and decorating Mrs Santa
Using red fabric, make a large sized skirt and bodice with kimono sleeves as described on pages 19-21. Make long sleeves, and finish the lower edge of the sleeves with broder lace and a 5 mm ($^3/_{16}$") ruffle

Knitted hat
Using white and 3.25 mm (No 10) needles, cast on 30sts.

Work 6 rows rib (3 ridges). Break off white and change to red.

Work 12 rows st st, starting with a knit row.

Next row: K, *K2tog, K4*, rep from * – * four more times (25 sts).

Next row: P.

Rep last 2 rows, always working 1st less between dec, until 5sts rem on needle.

Break off yarn. Thread yarn end through rem 5sts, draw up and fasten off. Close centre back seam.

Apron
Making 5 mm ($^3/_{16}$") seams and double hems, hem the two short sides and one long side of the apron skirt. Gather the remaining long (top) side to measure about 7 cm (3"). With right sides together and raw edges even, sew one long side of the waistband over the gathered top edge of the apron. Fold the waistband double, turn all sides in 5 mm ($^3/_{16}$"), and sew the other long side against the back over the previous seam. Sew waist-ties to each end of the waistband on the wrong side. Hem two long and one short (top) side of the apron-bib. Sew the bib-ties to the wrong side of each top corner of the bib. Matching their centres, position the apron over the top edge of the red skirt, and slide the bib underneath for 2 cm ($^3/_4$"). Glue the apron over the bib and remaining skirt edge, bringing the ties around the waist towards the back. Cross over the two bib-ties at the back, trim surplus ribbon, and glue ends to the wrong sides of the apron ties. Knot the apron ties into a bow at centre back, making small loops and long ends.

Dress
Sew Christmas lace along the lower edge of the skirt on the right side. For the collar, cut a piece of broder cotton lace to fit around the neck, adding 5 mm ($^3/_{16}$") for hem at the ends. Hem the ends. Fold the long raw side under 5 mm

Mrs Santa wears a dress and apron sewn from cotton fabrics, and a charming hat knitted from 8-ply wool. These 20 cm (8") dolls make a cheerful Christmas decoration

($^{3}/_{16}$"), and work a row of small running stitches closely along the folded edge. Place the collar around the neck from centre front to centre front, draw up to fit the neck, and fasten off. Glue a button between the two sides of the collar at the front.

Hat
Glue the large pompom to the pointed end of the hat. Glue the hat to the head. Bring the pointed end over towards the right side and sew the crease lightly in place. Glue the holly leaves and small bow to the right side of the hat.

Decorations in hands
Bend the arms and hands into a realistic position (see the photograph). Glue Christmas greenery in the left arm against the waist. Place a small amount of polyester fibre filling inside the basket and glue the white bear on top.

Glue the basket over the doll's left hand, and the wreath over the right arm.

Glasses
Keeping about 2 cm ($^{3}/_{4}$") of each end of the wire straight, twist wire around a pencil to form two circles about 1 cm ($^{3}/_{8}$") apart. Flatten and bend each circle sideways, so they will lie just below the straight ends. Stick the ends of the wire into the head underneath the hair, with the circles positioned over the eyes.

15: SNOWMAN

Finished size
20 cm (8") including hat

Materials
About 40g 8-ply white yarn
Small quantities 8-ply yarn in black and red
3.25 mm (No 10) knitting needles
2.50 mm crochet hook
Large-eyed tapestry needle
4 cm (1½") diameter white foam ball
Polyester fibre filling
Strong cardboard circle 5.5 cm (2¼") in diameter
Crocheted circle 5.5 cm (2¼") in diameter
Clear-drying glue
3 black pompoms 6 mm (¼") in diameter
2 cm (¾") red toadstool and two 4 cm (1½") pieces of
    Christmas greenery, tied together with a bow of 3 mm
    (⅛") red ribbon
10 cm x 7.5 mm (4" x ¼") red taffeta ribbon
Four or five 10 cm (4") branches of fine Christmas green-
    ery tied together with a bow of 3 mm (⅛") red ribbon
For the gift box , 10 cm x 12 cm (4" x 5") strong cardboard;
    tape; thin red fabric 14 cm (5½") square; gold cord

Pattern for Snowman
Following the pattern below, assemble and finish the snowman as described on pages 13-19, but omit hair and petticoat, and work eyes in black and mouth in red, using knitting yarn. Sew white seams with white yarn, and black seams
with black yarn.

Body
Using white and 3.25 mm (No 10) needles, cast on 32sts.
Work 4 rows rib (2 ridges).
Work 36 rows st st, starting with a knit row.

Head
Next row: K, and dec 3sts evenly across row (29 sts).
Work 15 rows st st, starting with a purl row.
Next row: *K2tog*; rep to end of row (15 sts).
Next row: *K2tog*; rep to end of row (8 sts).
Break off yarn, thread yarn end through rem sts, draw up
    and fasten off.

Arms
Make 2. Using black and 3.25 mm (No 10) needles, cast on
    5sts.
1st row: K, and inc 1st in each st (10 sts).
Work 5 rows rib (3 ridges). Break off black and change to
    white.
Work 20 rows st st, starting with a knit row. Cast off.

Crocheted circle
Work a 5.5 cm (2¼") diameter white circle, following in-
    structions on page 15.

Crocheted hat
Using black and 2.50 mm hook, work 4ch, close into a ring
    with a sl st.
1st rnd: 8dc in ring. Use a safety-pin, or tie a small piece of
    coloured thread through work, to indicate the first stitch
    of the next rnd, and move this at the beginning of each
    following rnd.
2nd rnd (and all other rnds): Work in back of loop of sts,
    2dc in each dc (16 sts).
3rd rnd: *1dc, 2dc in next dc*; rep from * – * to end of rnd
    (24 sts).
4th-13th rnds: 1dc in each dc.
14th rnd (brim of hat): *1tr in next dc, 2tr in next dc*; rep
    from * – * to end of row.
15th rnd: 1dc in each st. Fasten off.

Knitted scarf
Using red and 3.25 mm (No 10) needles, cast on 5 sts.
Work a 25 cm (10") scarf in rib, alternating 2 rows red and
2 rows white, and ending with two rows red. To make a
tassel, loop two red and two white 8 cm (3") pieces of yarn
around the ends of the scarf. Wind a piece of red yarn 5
mm (³/₁₆") down from the looped top (also catching the yarn
ends left over from casting on) to form a tassel. Trim excess
yarn to make a 3 cm (1¼") tassel.

Decorating
Glue three pompoms evenly spaced to the front body.
Knot the scarf around the neck. Glue the hat over the
head. Push the top in slightly, and turn the brim upwards
around the face. Glue red ribbon around the brim of the

This handsome snowman is 20 cm (8") high, and wears a stylish hat and a smart long scarf. He makes a wonderful decoration after the Christmas gift (perhaps jewellery or a banknote) has been retrieved from the parcel in his hand

hat, overlapping the ends. Glue the toadstool decoration on top of the ribbon on one side of the hat, following the photograph . Glue the branches of Christmas greenery with red bow to the inside of one arm. Pin or glue the small parcel (see method below) to the other hand.

Square parcel
Copy the pattern onto strong cardboard. Cut out along the solid lines, and score the broken lines. Fold four sections upwards to form a box, and join the corners using tape. Insert a gift or banknote, and fold the lid section over. Wrap the box with thin red fabric and gold cord tied into a bow.

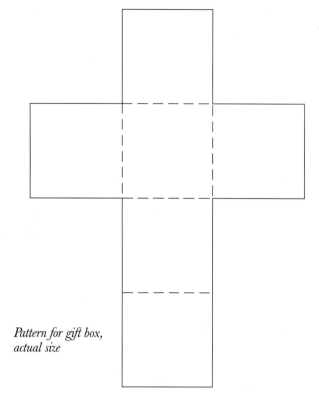

Pattern for gift box, actual size

16: SMALL HANGING ANGEL

Finished size

12 cm (5")

Materials

One small doll with legs (see page 15), with features and basic hairstyle; replace the bloomers with a petticoat made from one layer of 3 cm (1¼") lace

15 cm x 115 cm (6" x 45") white dotted pale blue thin fabric

Matching coloured sewing thread

Tracing paper

Pencil and ruler

Clear-drying glue

20 cm x 1 cm (8" x ³⁄₈") white gathered lace

30 cm x 7.5 mm (12" x ¼") blue braid with white flowers

10 cm x 5 mm (4" x ³⁄₁₆") gold braid

20 cm x 3 mm (8" x ⅛") pale blue ribbon

1.25 cm (½") diameter golden bell

4 cm (1½") piece of fine Christmas greenery

Double-sided gold cardboard 10 cm (4") square

20 cm (8") gold cord for the hanger

Dressing and decorating

Using dotted blue fabric, make a small sized bodice with kimono sleeves, extending the bottom far enough to form a long dress. Cut down the centre back far enough for the doll's head to fit through. Close the split, sew the centre of a piece of blue ribbon over the lower end, and tie it into a bow. Hem the dress to leave about 2.5 cm (1") of the doll's legs visible. Finish the lower edge of the sleeves with lace and a 5 mm (³⁄₁₆") ruffle.

Sew flower braid along the hemline on the right side. For the collar, cut a piece of lace to fit around the neck edge, adding 5 mm (³⁄₁₆") hem allowance each end and sewing it down. Sew the collar around the neck edge from centre back to centre back. Glue a circle of flower braid over the head, and glue a circle of gold braid outside the flower braid. Lace the bell onto a short end of white sewing thread, and knot the ends together. Bend the arms forward and sew the tips of the hands together, taking in the knotted end of the bell hanger. Glue a piece of Christmas greenery over the tips of the hands.

Trace the wing pattern onto tracing paper, copy onto gold cardboard and cut out. Fold the wings outwards on the dotted lines. Glue the centre of the wing to the centre back of the angel. Glue the hanger against the base of the head.

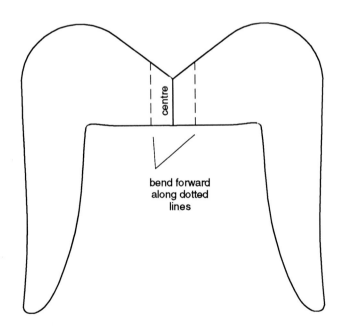

Pattern for angel's wings, actual size

74

This whimsical tree decoration is about 12 cm (5") high, and can be quickly made as a loving gift

17: INSPIRATIONS

The glory box

This beautiful doll is worked the same way as the mother from Teatime in the Nursery (page 54) but is decorated differently. The apron is made the same way as the Little Goose Girl's apron (page 26) but the ribbon ties are knotted at the front

The last waltz

Three exquisite dolls, dressed in taffeta, on a wooden base with a flower arch. The dolls are worked the same way as the mother from Teatime in the Nursery (page 54), but are more lavishly decorated with pearls, flowers and feathers. Each doll carries a crocheted reticule, worked from the pattern in Fairy Godmothers on page 51. The pink doll's basic hairstyle (page 17) is decorated with feathers, and she stands on a pedestal under a flower arch worked the same way as the arch from Here Comes the Bride on page 43

Off to the garden party

This adorable doll is worked in the same way as the Flower Seller and Self-portrait dolls (see pages 33 and 24), but is slightly taller, the knitted body being extended to make her 18 cm (7") high. She wears an elegant straw hat decorated with roses, and carries a precious beaded bag in one hand

Friends forever

Two cheerful little mates taking a stroll — perhaps they are off to the movies! The dolls are worked the same way as the small doll from the group At the Country Fair (page 36), but have slightly taller knitted bodies, being 15 cm (6") high. One doll has the plaits over the ears hairstyle (page 19) and holds a small flocked kangaroo. The other doll has one plait over the head (page 18), and carries a shoulder bag crocheted from red DMC No 8 Coton Perle

Precious memories

Here is Claire's latest creation, worked in her ninetieth year! A precious doll with a small framed photograph of Claire and her beloved mother Gertrud, taken in 1915. The doll is worked the same way as the dolls from Maypole Dance on page 29, but differently decorated. She carries a bag made from a 6.5 cm x 2.5 cm (2¹⁄₂"x 1") rectangle worked in double crochet, using white DMC No 8 Coton Perle. The golden necklace is made from a bracelet charm

INDEX